The Church in Areas of Conflict

Other titles in this series

Laos: No Turning Back

The Church in Areas of Conflict

Central America
Into the Crossfire

Edited by Dale W Kietzman

Marshalls

Marshalls Paperbacks
Marshall Morgan & Scott
3 Beggarwood Lane, Basingstoke, Hants, RG23 7LP, UK

Copyright © 1985 by Dale W Kietzman
First published in 1985 by Marshall Morgan & Scott Ltd in
conjunction with Open Doors International.

ISBN 0 551 01248 X

Typeset by Brian Robinson, North Marston, Bucks.
Printed in Great Britain by
Anchor Brendon Ltd, Tiptree, Colchester

Contents

A word of explanation

This volume has been specifically written to communicate something of what Christians are experiencing in an area of conflict, in this case Central America. While some information is provided about the historical development and cultural aspects of Central America, the goal has been to discuss the current situation of believers in the five countries that are in focus. Most of the reporting, therefore, recounts selected events since 1980.

The various chapters have been written primarily on the basis of the experience of Open Doors staff members, who have spent months of travel in Central America, during which they have investigated and reported (and continue to do so) the problems Christians face there.

We recommend two general reference works which give more complete historical and statistical data on the Church in Central America:

Holland, Clifton L (ed.), *Central America and the Caribbean*, vol. 4 of *World Christianity* (Monrovia, California: Missions Advanced Research and Communications, 1981)

Barrett, David B (ed.), *World Christian Encyclopedia*, (New York; Oxford: Oxford University Press, 1982)

Contributors to this volume

Brother Andrew is the founder and president of Open Doors International. He first began to travel to areas where the Church lives under restriction when he visited Poland in 1955. He has since travelled throughout the world, encouraging Christian brothers living in areas of conflict and persecution, and carrying news of their welfare to the Church in the free world. His personal ministry has included all of Central America.

Peter Asael Gonzalez, a well known Spanish language communicator, is the speaker on 'Al Punto', a daily radio broadcast heard throughout Latin America. He is the author (with Dan Wooding) of *Prophets of Revolution* (London: Hodder & Stoughton, 1982), a book about his own family's experience in responding to the political tension and social changes in America. In his remarkable family, one brother helped in a literacy campaign in Nicaragua; another is organising co-operatives in Mexico; a sister is writing books about fighting injustice. They are all 'prophets of revolution', motivated by a burning Christian faith, but finding different ways to serve Him in a context of devastating social and political upheaval.

Dale W Kietzman, an anthropologist and Latin American specialist, was a missionary with Wycliffe Bible Translators for 27 years, serving in Mexico, Peru and Brazil. He developed the Latin America regional staff for Open Doors and more recently has served as Open Doors' Director of International Development.

J.W. Meyer has been covering Central America for several years. Raised and educated in Latin America, Meyer has unusual insights into the developing situations in many Latin countries. The perspectives presented are provocative, but are based on first-hand information in all cases.

Dan Wooding is an award-winning British journalist who co-authored *Prophets of Revolution* with Peter Gonzalez. As director of the *Open Doors News Service,* he has travelled frequently in all countries of Central America. He is the author of some eighteen books.

Introduction

by Brother Andrew

Last year I had a chance encounter with a group of guerrillas in the remote rebel-held village of Sesori in northern El Salvador. We had gone there to film a segment for a television documentary called 'Children of Revolution'.

As we came into the village, we noticed boys as young as fourteen walking casually across the village square, with rifles slung over their shoulders and freshly stocked ammunition belts wrapped around their slim waists.

My interpreter asked one of them, Roberto, to talk with me. This fifteen-year-old carefully adjusted his black beret before answering my first question.

'Do you know who Jesus Christ is?' I asked.

'You mean God, as they say', was Roberto's quick reply. I nodded, then pointed to the church across the street.

'Do you go to church?'

'Yes, sometimes', said Roberto.

Other guerrillas, both men and women, were drawn toward the spectacle of a foreign television crew in this isolated village. The serious faces of civilians, who kept to the background, gave away the fear and concern they felt over the guerrillas' presence in the town.

'Roberto,' I asked, 'do you ever read the Bible?'

Roberto paused. 'The truth is that the Bible doesn't really suit us. We have to fight the war with our guns. Perhaps later, when we've won the war, maybe we'll read the Bible.'

That is one of my deepest concerns for Central America. Too many of its people are seeking for answers in other ideologies, and enforcing their ideas with violence. While we call the people 'Christians', there is little concern for the teachings of Christ, especially when He said, 'I am the way, the truth and the life; no one can come to the Father except by Me.'

Unfortunately, the majority of those who are fighting the larger and smaller wars in Central America are under twenty years of age and are already thoroughly convinced that they are fighting for a just cause. For young people like Roberto, the ideology of the civil strife and violence that surrounds them daily has robbed them of any possibility of enjoying their teenage years. It is as remote as is a peaceful solution to their country's problems.

In the meeting in Los Angeles at which we launched the co-ordinated plan for youth evangelism through the churches of Latin America, called 'Young Continent for Christ', I told the Latin Christian leaders and representatives of mission organisations working there that our job as leaders with a vision for Latin America is to hear what God is saying, even in the midst of the noise and violence around us.

We need to pay attention to the voice of God, not just to what He said in the past, but to what God is saying today about the times in which we live, and about the future which all of us inevitably face. For what happens in Central America will affect all of Latin America; and if we fail to support our Christian brothers there in their hour of suffering, we will weaken the cause of the Church around the world.

There will be no revival, no blessing, and no outpouring of the Holy Spirit unless there is a large enough group of people willing to pay the price. If such people can be found today only in countries where there is active persecution and restriction, such as in China, Russia, Poland and Romania—countries where revival is indeed taking place—then we should be willing to say, 'Lord God, let restrictions come here; start the persecution with me!'

Then, you see, I am no longer fighting against something like 'the revolution', but my stand, my complete dedication, will be to the thing I am *for*: faith in Jesus Christ.

That is the only way we can convince the young population of Central America. That is the way our enemy operates. He offers nothing to his disciples but blood, sweat and tears . . . and loss of life.

But how can we reach them? One of the Open Doors staff once asked President Efrain Rios Montt why so many young people seemed to identify with the terrorists.

His reply? 'Because there is no alternative to their cause. The problem is that the youth are so manipulated that we make them responsible for everything. And we point our finger at the youth. But that is only one finger; I have three pointing back at me. I am responsible for the youth, but I don't have the capacity for such a responsibility. I tell them what to do, but I don't do what I tell them to do. This is the anguish, all because we don't know Christ.'

Yes, we need to preach a radical message. The more radical you preach the Gospel imperative, the stronger the followers you will get. The harder you make the choice, the more dedicated they—those who have to choose—will be. The more you stress that this is a battle, a life or death struggle, in which the whole Church worldwide is involved, the more they will want to be with you in the battle.

And then they, in their turn, will bear fruit as they come to grips with the real issues of life. Let's get the young people fired up! There are many who are willing to suffer and are prepared to make sacrifices. So let's be clear in our message; let them know what price they must pay.

If there is anything that Open Doors can do to spread this message throughout the whole of Central America, then it will be helping to bring equality within the Body of Jesus Christ worldwide. Because God is righteous; He will not allow His Body to grow—or to suffer—out of proportion. Persecution and world evangelisation go hand in hand.

Right now we should concentrate all of our efforts and all of our prayer concern on Central America. The believers in these countries are in cross-fire. Unless they can draw strength from the whole Body of Christ worldwide, they may not be able to survive the difficult days ahead of them.

We need to help our brothers and sisters in Central America to seize the opportunities of this hour: the 'open doors' that are uniquely open to them. But they need our full attention, our understanding, our prayers and all the help we can give.

1: Into the cauldron

By Peter Asael Gonzalez with Dan Wooding

A sudden ear-splitting explosion ripped through the dusk of violence-torn San Salvador, followed by a cloud of billowing black smoke.

'The hotel's been bombed', I shouted to my journalist companion, Dan Wooding. My heart began to pound unmercifully in my chest. I'd been through guerrilla attacks like this before and realised there could be more explosions.

The blast blew out all the windows on one side of the hotel. When no more explosions followed the first, we joined scores of people rushing to see what had happened. Overseas TV crews who had been drinking in the bar were already outside, their equipment ready to film.

As we surveyed the devastation, both Dan and I noticed a cluster of well dressed young men standing apart, discussing something urgently. Then one of them approached Dan.

'Are you a journalist?' he asked in reasonably good English.

Dan nodded.

'Would you like to know why we planted the bomb?'

Dan nodded again, not quite knowing how to react.

'Well, you see, the attorney who has this office,' he

15

said, pointing to the mangled remains of the building located across from the hotel, 'this man was on television earlier this afternoon, criticising the terrorists. We decided to teach him a lesson and so we left a package for him on his doorstep.'

Dan was obviously dumbstruck by this open admission of responsibility.

'Would you like a tour of the area where we have planted bombs in the last few days? I'd feel honoured to show you around.'

While my British friend had been concentrating on this modern-day urban guerrilla, I was desperately trying to catch his eye to warn him to get out of the situation as quickly as possible. He seemed on the verge of agreeing to make this highly dangerous tour in the capital of 'the land of the smoking gun.'

Finally Dan looked at me. My whole face said. 'Get out of this, and get out right now!'

We picked our way through the twisted metal and broken glass to the hotel and went back up to our room.

'Let's pray for that young terrorist,' I suggested. 'He sees nothing wrong in planting bombs and then giving interviews to the press afterward. He is so convinced that his cause is right, that he is willing to maim and kill for it.'

We were soon on our knees by our beds in that hotel room. We interceded for that young revolutionary and for all of the young people in this tragic land. We prayed that they would look for solutions other than those of the bomb and the bullet.

Afterwards, I looked at my friend—his face was still pale from the shock of the bomb blast—and I said, 'Do you know that this is the only country in the world that takes its name after our Lord?' El Salvador quite literally means, 'The Saviour'.

'How ironic that it is being crucified by a bloodbath of violence from both the left and the right.

'But it has not always been like this.' Indeed, I had to pinch myself to realise how Central America, which is one of the most beautiful regions of the world, had changed since I first began travelling through it back in 1964.

'But surely you as a Latin, Peter, must have seen the writing on the wall, even then,' said Wooding. 'You knew all about the huge gap between rich and poor, having had to shine shoes yourself as a boy in Monterrey just to help out your own family.'

I smiled, remembering those days. I was one of a large family of four brothers and four sisters, and it was a real struggle for our parents to provide for us. We were poor, true, but one thing we were constantly told was that we were part of a 'Royal Family'. Mama especially drummed this into us and, one by one, through her faithful prayers for us, we each were adopted into 'God's Royal Family', by making our own personal commitments to Him.

I remember those peaceful days of growing up in northern Mexico, going to school, getting my first job, meeting beautiful Blanca in church, even following her all the way down to Tampico, just to see her for a few hours.

Then, after a period at Bible seminary, we joined the Latin America Mission and Blanca and I moved down to San Jose, Costa Rica, to work in their publication company, Editorial Caribe. San Jose was a haven, but while we were there something happened that I believe was a portent of the future. John F Kennedy was visiting the country when Mount Irazu erupted, spewing out its red-hot lava and ashes. It

17

seemed to me at the time that something similar was about to happen in this part of the world: an explosion of violence. But in that green and peaceful world, it was easy to put such thoughts aside.

Of course, President Kennedy's blockade of the revolutionary island of Cuba at that same time was bringing worldwide attention to Latin America. After Fidel Castro's revolution in 1959, the Soviet Union had begun to look upon Cuba as its personal territory. They even tried to install missiles that could be used against the United States. Kennedy's strong action had persuaded Soviet leader Nikita Krushchev to back off, and the world turned its attention to other, more distant trouble spots.

Subsequently, while working with the United Bible Societies all over Latin America, I had become alarmed at the fragmentation of the Church in Central America. For instance, in Guatemala I discovered there are a staggering 200 denominations; and that in a country of eight million people. El Salvador has some 80 denominations, while Nicaragua has at least 75.

Eventually my consuming passion had turned to efforts directed toward uniting the church of Jesus Christ in Latin America. I became the director for the continent of the John 17: 21 Movement, which took its ideals from that verse which reads, 'That they all may be one; as thou, Father, art in me, and I in thee, that they also may be in us; that the world may believe that thou has sent me.'

It was during a visit to Managua, the capital of Nicaragua, in June 1979, that the reality of violence flooded in on me. I was in Managua to try and bring denominational leaders together to get to know and love each other. There were all sorts of reports about guerrilla activity out in the countryside, but I had not yet become conscious of the fact that something terrible was happening in Central America: the beginning of bloodshed that was to tear families apart throughout the region and bring the superpowers into this arena in a deadly struggle for supremacy.

In June 1979, the government of Anastasio Somoza was already in its death throes. Somoza and his family had ruled over Nicaraguan affairs with an iron fist for some forty-five years, and his father and brother had preceded Anastasio as president. The dynasty had enriched itself by hundreds of millions of dollars, had secured ownership of over a quarter of the cultivatable land, and had come to own the national airline and steamship company, as well as eighty-five other industrial establishments.

I had checked into a hotel on the edge of town, and was gazing out of the window of the room with Shaun, my Irish companion, when there was a sudden blinding barrage of rocket shells, quickly followed by the chatter of machine-gun fire. A cloud of billowing black smoke obscured the lovely violet of dusk.

I yelled at Shaun to 'close the curtains, switch off the lights, and get under the bed!' I guess I was already there! I knew that the area around the hotel was being attacked by the Sandinistas. (The Sandinista Front of National Liberation—FSLN—was named after a Nicaraguan national hero, Augusto Cesar Sandino, who was assassinated in 1934.)

At this time, the Sandinistas, a loose coalition of Marxists and non-Marxist Social Democrats, were pressing home their advantage against Somoza's storm troopers, the National Guard. Even while I rode in from the airport with Shaun, an Irish Christian I had met at the airport and who had offered

19

to share his room with me, I had seen the results of their attacks: tumbled telephone and electrical poles and shredded wires. Roadblocks were everywhere, quickly put up by FSLN supporters, who would pull up thousands of pavement bricks in their determination to defend their neighbourhoods against Somoza's bloody National Guard.

Having known poverty in my childhood in Mexico, it was easy to be sympathetic with the Nicaraguan people in their struggle for freedom. But as I was now plunged into the reality of their revolution, I knew I might soon become a bullet-riddled victim of it. Everything began to blur around that one preoccupation of staying alive.

As I listened to the frightening sound of exploding bombs, I recalled Lenin's phrase, 'The purpose of terror is to terrify.' It was certainly working in my case.

I was cotton-mouthed with fear as I began to pray from the strange vantage point of under the bed. 'Lord,' I said in a trembling voice, 'We are in your hands. If it is your will, I'm ready to die, but if you don't mind, I'd rather stay alive.'

From under his bed, I heard Shaun give a thin, nervous chuckle as he listened to my petition. I began to let my whirling thoughts zero in on my family. The image of Blanca, my beautiful wife, was clearly in front of me, outlined in every detail in the darkness: her deep hazel eyes, her ebony hair.

I felt tears sting my eyes as I asked the Lord, 'What will happen to her, or my four children, if I die, Lord? Who will take care of them?'

But in the hours I spent under that bed, I realised once again that if I was going to serve the people of Latin America, it might cost me my life. That was not a new thought to me, because I had faced mobs before. But then it had been a matter of misguided religious zeal; now it was generalised, senseless and meaningless violence.

Shaun sensed my unease and began fumbling under his bed. He managed to switch on a torch he had with him and then to flick through his Bible. When he came to Matthew 10: 28, he read out loud: 'And fear not them which kill the body, but are not able to kill the soul: but rather fear him which is able to destroy both soul and body in hell.'

Then Shaun turned to another verse, Psalm 116: 15, and read it to me: 'Precious in the sight of the Lord is the death of His saints.'

He paused briefly as if to allow those words to sink in. Then he said in a quiet voice, 'Peter, if we die we will go to be with Him. Surely that isn't so terrible, is it?'

I had to agree and felt not a little shamefaced that this young Christian was giving me such mature advice. After all, I had been a believer for some twenty years and it should have been the other way around!

As another bomb shook the whole hotel, I whispered across to my under-the-bed companion, 'Shaun, this area of the world used to be so happy-go-lucky. People had smiles. Now all I see are fearful faces, and all I hear is gunfire. It's hard to understand what is going on. There are so many troubles all over.'

Since I joined Open Doors in 1980, I have seen violence spread even farther through Central America. You would think all Latin Americans would now recognise a 'clear and present' danger. But to persuade some Christian leaders that their country is in serious trouble and that they should immediately start training their people to stand in the midst of

21

persecution, whether it should come from the right or the left is another matter indeed.

I remember taking Dutch-born Brother Andrew, known to the world as 'God's Smuggler', to El Salvador, blood-soaked after another military coup. He was anxious to meet Christians in the capital of San Salvador, but was disturbed when he found that none of them seemed to take seriously the implications of the turmoil in their country.

One pastor looked into Brother Andrew's clear blue eyes and declared: 'We know El Salvador well. Better than you. There will be no problems for believers here. It will never happen here.'

Our little group, which also included Brother Andrew's long-standing friend, Johan Companjen, himself a missionary to Vietnam before the fall of that country, looked at each other blankly. I could see that Brother Andrew was concerned with their smugness.

That evening the newspapers carried a bold, terrifying headline: 'Estado de Sitio' (State of Siege).

I read the article out loud to Andrew and Johan. 'It says here that the military have, today, introduced a 6 p.m. curfew. Anyone caught on the streets after that time could be shot. Apparently the new government has abandoned all civil rights. And we will have to forget about the evening's meeting.'

During the afternoon, we took a taxi ride around San Salvador. The taxi driver often had his foot to the floor as the cab screeched around the streets. He didn't want to get caught up in trouble!

As the smell of burning rubber came from underneath the cab, and we hurtled around another bend in the road, moving away from a large school complex, the driver shouted to us, 'Hey, did you hear about the massacre on that corner earlier today?'

We shook our heads in unison.

'The National Guard went in and killed a lot of students for demonstrating. We are on the verge of civil war. It looks as though what happened in Nicaragua could happen here.'

Next morning, a small group of ashen-faced pastors arrived at the hotel to meet with us. This time only six turned up.

Their spokesman was clearly shaken by what had happened. He began, 'Brothers, we have an apology to make to you. First of all, none of the other brothers could come because they feel the streets are too dangerous for them to be out. And second, we were wrong yesterday. We said that persecution could never happen here. Now we can see the warning signs clearly.'

There was an awkward pause, then he added, 'What can you do to help us? We really do want our people to be more than conquerors in this terrible situation.'

Since that time, we have been active in training Christian leaders and lay people all over Central America in 'Survival and Victory' seminars, using techniques that have also been taught in Southeast Asia, Africa, and other areas where Christians are confronting situations of increasing violence and repression. We don't just want the Church to survive; we want all of the believers to be able to live victoriously.

We know that the peaceful, almost bucolic Central America that many of us knew is a thing of the past. Now the area is like a cauldron that is getting hotter and hotter.

But isn't that just where we should be? I believe we should all want to become prophets in the midst of revolution. And the only weapon we should use is

God's Word, which cuts closer than a two-edged sword. We should come to them with love, not hate! Will you march with us?

2: The Central American heritage

By Dale W Kietzman

Central America is that twisting neck of land that connects North America with South America. It extends some 1200 miles from the Gulf of Tehuantepec in southern Mexico to the borders of Colombia.

This gradually narrowing isthmus, running more west to east than it does north to south, connects the two Americas. It is extremely mountainous; high plateaus provide temperate climates for its larger cities; the lengthy coastlines hold hundreds of isolated tropical beaches.

Seven countries, plus a part of Mexico, have been carved out of the isthmus, but only five have traditionally been labelled as Central America: Guatemala, Honduras, El Salvador, Nicaragua and Costa Rica.

Belize, known through most of its history as British Honduras, has few cultural links with its Spanish neighbours. It is more closely identified with the English-speaking Caribbean, from which a majority of its people came. It gained its independence only in this decade, in sharp contrast with the historical development of the other nations of Central America.

Although linked geographically to the Central American nations, Panama also has an entirely different political and economic history. It was severed from Colombia only in 1903, under the pressures of completing the inter-ocean canal. Panama now is often identified with Central American issues, but it also has unique relationships and a church history that makes it difficult to include in generalisations about Central America.

Mexico, while traditionally not listed as a part of Central America, is very closely linked by history, language, culture and religion. Today it receives the spill-over of the troubles in the region in the tens of thousands of refugees that move northward each year.

The Indian civilisations of pre-Colombian Central America are shadowed in mystery. Monumental cities and temple sites are overgrown with jungle. Inscriptions are all but erased by erosion. Archaeological finds of enormous importance have been removed to decorate private homes.

Perhaps the greatest of all native American cultures was the Mayan, which left its impress over much of Guatemala and southern Mexico. This civilisation had developed a calendar far more accurate than that used by the Spaniards at the time of the conquest. Only they and the Hindus, from whom we inherited the decimal system, had discovered the use of the zero. Their remarkable architecture allowed the construction of high-rise buildings, using the offset principle.

In the first Christian millenium, the Maya were building cities in the Yucatan, in the jungle areas of what is now Mexico, Guatemala and Honduras. They eventually were spread over an area of 125,000 square miles, the most brilliant civilisation of the New World.

South of the limit of the Mayan culture, most of the tribes of Central America were shifting cultivators, and their population was much more scattered through the highlands.

The sixteenth century Spanish conquerors burned Mayan codices in what they thought was an attack on paganism. The Maya retreated to their last strongholds in the jungles of Guatemala, their civilisation in ruins, its existence to be forgotten for centuries.

John Lloyd Stephens, a nineteenth century diplomat travelling in Central America, discovered the lost city of Copan, the Mayan astronomical centre in northern Honduras. His account aroused scientific interest in the Maya people and their accomplishments:

> It lay before us like a shattered bark in the midst of the ocean, her masts gone, her name effaced, her crew perished, and none to tell us whence she came, to whom she belonged, how long on her voyage, or what caused her destruction—her lost people to be traced only by fancied resemblance in the construction of the vessel, and, perhaps, never to be known at all.*

The Maya had actually organised themselves into city states much like those of ancient Greece. The ceremonial life of the city states was elaborate, the prosperity of the country flowing into them. The Maya excelled in architecture, sculpture, painting, hieroglyphic writing, astronomy and mathematics.

The cities were surrounded by cornfields. Everything

*John Lloyd Stephens: *Incidents of Travel in Central America, Chiapas, and Yucatan*, edited by Richard L Fredmore, 2 vols. (New Brunswick: Rutgers University Press, 1949. vol. 1, p 81).

27

the Maya believed in was related to the crops. An elaborate theology involved propitiating the gods in order to receive abundant harvests. The cycle of corn fixed his calendar and the rhythm of life.

Over the centuries the ceremonials became more complicated. The religion, however, remained very personal and touched the entire cycle of life. The destiny of each person, the time for each major event in life, depended on astrology and the gods.

The Maya universe was caught in a never-ending struggle between the powers of good and evil. Good meant rain, fertility and abundance; bad brought drought, storms and hunger. These conditions extended on into a final paradise and hell.

A supreme creator God was too remote from life to make his worship efficacious. Instead there were hundreds of gods and goddesses, one to affect each condition of life.

The days of Mayan splendour disappeared with the conquest, but the descendants of these people are the principal stock of the Central American population, especially in the more heavily inhabited mountain areas of the north. And through them, many of these ancient beliefs—and ancient gods—live on.

Today, peasants in the mountains of Guatemala still seek out the tribal incense priests, who offer sacrifices and do *costumbre*. He is the only one who can speak to the evil spirits and to the gods of each mountain. He can appease these gods and bring good harvests and strong families. From many little shrines on mountainsides come his prayers:

O spirit that lives in this place.
O spirit that lives in the end of the hill.

O spirit that lives under the hill.
O spirit of the prince of this world, have patience,
have patience.
O you who inhabit this place, this is my payment,
this is my gift.
O you who inhabit this cliff,
O spirit of the shadow of the pine tree.
O prince of this world,
    we beg our help from you,
    we beg our life from you;
    for this reason we cry here in the world.
O world that always exists.
Owner of the world.
Miraculous one.
One spirit of this world,
    forgive me.
O everlasting world,
    forgive me.
    Remember your son,
    remember our children,
    forgive our sins.
O spirit of the world that always exists.*

The dominant motive of the Spanish conquistadors
who occupied Central America, as in other areas of
Latin America, was to find El Dorado'wealth in the
form of gold and silver already accumulated by Indian
civilisations. Lacking that, the manpower of large
Indian populations was essential for mining or other
ventures that would bring quick profits.

The Spaniards were also deeply intent on estab-
lishing their kind of civilisation and their religion in

*Prayer of an Aguacateco incense priest recorded in the film made
in Guatemala by Wycliffe Bible Translators, entitled,
'Unsheathed'.

the New World. They had a genuine, even fanatical, zeal for the spread of the Christian faith. They established universities (the University of Mexico has had an uninterrupted existence since 1563), set up printing presses, and in various ways promoted the arts.

One of the first results of the arrival of the Spaniards was the devastating spread of European diseases among the Indians. In some areas, whole populations were wiped out within the first decades of the conquest.

Still, the native population always outnumbered the Spaniards, because relatively few people were actually involved in the colonisation. During the whole colonial period, only about 300,000 registered immigrants left Spain, destined for Mexico and Central America.

The result of this numerical imbalance in much of the area was that the Europeans freely intermarried with native Indians. Where large Indian populations existed before, as in Guatemala, today there is a large proportion of people with Indian ancestors, but, because they no longer identify as Indians, they are termed *ladino*.

In Honduras, El Salvador and Nicaragua, where the native populations were scanty and scattered, the Indian contribution to the present day population is relatively smaller. In Costa Rica it is almost non-existent, because the tribes were hostile or were soon wiped out by the ravages of disease.

Costa Rica, in fact, had a different history of settlement to the rest of Central America. There were no gold mines to bring wealth, or Indian civilisations to Christianise. Costa Rica was the farthest outpost of the Captaincy-General of Guatemala. Its first settlers made a long trek in 1561 to establish themselves in the Meseta Central. In this isolated spot, the people became small pioneer-style farmers, raising or producing all they consumed. There was no aristocracy, no individuals who could claim special position or status. Perhaps this explains why Costa Rica today is the most enduring model of democracy in Latin America.

Central America historically was a part of the Viceroyalty of New Spain, established by Hernán Cortés and governed from Mexico City. The first expedition from Mexico reached the southern highlands in 1523, and the city of Antigua, founded in 1541, became the administrative centre for the Captaincy-General or Audiencia of Guatemala. This subdivision of New Spain included what is now the southern Mexican state of Chiapas, and the present-day republics of Guatemala, Honduras, El Salvador, Nicaragua and Costa Rica.

The history of Central America is thus linked with Mexico's until the early nineteenth century. When Mexico declared independence from Spain in 1821, the whole of Central America was included.

But in 1823, Guatemala declared independence from Mexico, and this included all of the old Captaincy-General of Guatemala, except Chiapas. The only purpose of the independence movement, which had been brewing for some time, appears to have been freedom from outside interference. Originally, the hostility was directed toward Spain; after 1821, it was directed toward Mexico; and after 1823, it was directed toward Guatemala City.

El Salvador was the first province in Central America to challenge Spanish rule. Father Jose Matias Delgado led an abortive uprising in 1811, followed by another in 1814. These sparked general unrest which resulted in the continued pressure for complete independence.

By 1839, both El Salvador and Nicaragua had withdrawn from the United Provinces of Central America, an attempt at a regional government with its capital in Guatemala. Honduras and Costa Rica followed suit, more because there was not much else to do than because of any immediate sense of nationality.

The five new countries began their independent existence with no specific ideologies concerning the role of the state. The large landowners and the military were in control, and they tended to perpetuate their hold on political offices. Thus, with the exception of Costa Rica, the countries were often governed by a succession of military-backed dictatorships.

In many ways over the past one hundred years, the United States and the foreign business interests identified with it, have supplanted Spain as the target of resentment fuelled by Central America's strong drive toward freedom from outside interference. Nothing has been as politically popular as an attack on the United Fruit Company, or on the intervention of the U.S. Marines in Nicaragua from 1912 to 1925 and 1926 to 1933, or frequent U.S. interference in close-by Cuba, governed under the Platt amendment until 1934.

New state ideologies are now developing in Central America. They are set in the context of a well developed sense of nationality, but they all also make use of the strong resentment toward outside tutelage, particularly from North America.

The Catholic church had introduced Christianity into Central America, and had a virtual monopoly on evangelisation and the control of religious education and activities until the late nineteenth century. Its only competition was with the old Indian religions, which now had developed into many local versions of Christo-paganism.

Due to a chronic shortage of Catholic priests and other religious workers, the people in the smaller towns and in rural villages were left to conduct their religious life with only occasional visits from the clergy. Through much of the area, a system of voluntary religious service developed, often referred to as a *cofradia*. This provided the leadership needed for organising and paying for local religious fiestas during the year.

Apparently the first establishment of regular Protestant worship in Central America occurred when foreign residents in San Jose, Costa Rica, began a house church in 1848. This eventually led to a church building in 1865.

In 1849, German Moravian missionaries had begun work along the Miskito coast of Nicaragua. The Methodists began work in Honduras in 1860, and the Presbyterians in Guatemala in 1882.

But the real invasion of Protestant missionaries, especially from North America, began with the formation of the Central American Mission in Texas. This group quickly entered all the Central American countries: Costa Rica in 1891, both Honduras and El Salvador in 1896, Guatemala in 1899 and Nicaragua in 1900.

This timing of the arrival of Protestant missions involved, in part, the changing status of the Catholic Church. The concept of the separation of church and state had not been a part of the independence ideology. The first Central American country to incorporate separation in its constitution was Guatemala in 1871. It had been heavily influenced by Mexico's example, and moved rather radically against the Catholic Church.

Honduras followed suit in 1880, El Salvador in 1886 and Nicaragua in 1893. Costa Rica still recognises the Catholic Church as the state church, and gives it many privileges not extended to Protestant denominations.

The Protestant churches grew slowly in the early decades of this century, working as they were among people who were loyal to the Catholic Church, but who were also very dependent on *cofradia*-type organisations, which typically integrated the social and political life of the community with the church.

Dramatic changes came only after World War II, and a series of more recent events have apparently encouraged more rapid church growth. These encouraging factors are listed variously, but include the improving public image of Evangelicals; the increasing literacy plus the emphasis on Bible reading among Catholics; the use of radio (and now television) for evangelism; and the changes that have taken place within the Catholic Church in the last two decades.

But church growth is an effect of evangelism, and evangelism is a response to commitment. The tremendous growth of evangelical faith now being documented in Central America is a testimony not to mission boards or external events, but to the new sense of commitment and dedication of Central American believers who recognise that they have another King, not of this world, nor to be discovered by the politics of this world. He is the One who should reign in heart and life.

3: Flashpoint in church growth

By Dan Wooding

I put my arm around the shoulder of the slightly-built president as our little group stood in a circle for a time of prayer. Throughout the session, the head of state murmured, 'Gloria a Dios' (Glory to God), a phrase that seemed to characterise this man who had become such an enigma to the world press.

Gathered in the presidential office of one of the world's most controversial leaders of that time were an international group of Christians that included the Dutch-born Brother Andrew, author of *God's Smuggler*; and Mexican-born Peter Gonzalez, author of *Prophets of Revolution*. As we praised the Lord together, armed guards stood yards away on the other side of the door, their automatic weapons ready for action.

Before this impromptu worship service, Guatemala's 'born-again' President Efrain Rios Montt, wearing a simple grey sports jacket, told us, 'I would be exhausted if I were the president, but I'm simply the servant of the Lord. He governs, He decides, He reigns.'

Montt then explained that he used his presidential position for evangelism by handing out Gideon Bibles to non-Christian visitors. He also spoke to the nation each Sunday night on television, sharing with the people his Christian convictions.

That year, 1983, was an extraordinary period in the history of Guatemala, a country the size of the state of New York, with a population of just under eight million. With the blessing of their power-base in the palace, evangelicals from overseas (mainly North America) moved in full force with ministers and missionaries, new churches, clinics, dental services, schools, even aid for low-cost housing.

'The only political party now active is evangelism,' a Guatemala City newspaper editor observed.

Rios Montt had come to power following a coup by young officers on March 23, 1982 and, in a country that is predominantly Roman Catholic, he had upset many Catholic leaders by moving into the palace, to be his 'advisors', two leading members of the charismatic Verbo (Word) church in Guatemala City, of which he was (and still is) a devoted member.

The church, which has its headquarters in Eureka, California, had initially sent representatives to Guatemala in 1976 to give aid to victims of one of Central America's frequent earthquakes. This one had devastated many areas in Guatemala, killing 24,000, injuring 77,000, destroying some 254,000 homes and leaving hundreds of thousands homeless.

The Eureka missionaries established a church in a tent in the capital city, and Rios Montt became their most celebrated convert. His sixteen months in the presidency perhaps marked the apex of unprecedented evangelical outreach and church growth in Guatemala, the most populous of the Central American republics.

As we left the ornate, turn-of-the-century presidential palace, I saw just across the street obvious signs of the North American invasion. Hundreds of volunteers from Youth With a Mission (YWAM) were handing out leaflets inviting local residents to a Christian rock concert in a nearby park.

The young 'missionaries' were following in the wake of the YWAM ship, the M.V. Anastasis (Greek for 'resurrection'). The ship had arrived in war-ravaged Guatemala to deliver nearly $600,000 (U.S.) worth of aid, as part of 'Operation Love Lift', for the mainly Indian population hit by the bloody guerrilla war that had been raging in the countryside for years.

The day I had arrived in Guatemala City, a high-powered delegation of Christian leaders also came in from the States. The group included Billy Graham's son, Franklin, who heads up Samaritan's Purse, an agency that supports relief efforts around the world. The visitors had dinner with the president and later were flown out to see some of the towns and villages now back in government control. They were able to see, firsthand, the 'bullets and beans' programme, a plan to feed the population and also arm the villagers against guerrilla attacks.

A media campaign was being waged by Rios Montt's government to tell the world that he was winning the war against the guerrillas and against corruption in his country. An equally well-orchestrated campaign was being waged by the four major guerrilla groups and their supporters, many of whom claim to be Christians, followers of 'liberation theology'.

It was not easy to discover what was really happening in Guatemala. Could Rios Montt, a military man, really reverse years of repression by the armed forces? Were the stories of massacres of Indians by the man his opponents dubbed the 'born-again butcher' really true?

37

A classified U.S. Government report filed by the U.S. Embassy in Guatemala City in 1982, since made public, concluded that a 'concentrated disinformation campaign' was waged 'against the Guatemalan government by groups supporting the communist insurgency in Guatemala'. This had 'enlisted the support of conscientious human rights and church organisations which may not fully appreciate that they are being utilised'.

Montt himself has said, 'Armies and swords are not God's means for bringing change, since God brings peaceful change by the work of the Holy Spirit.' That is why he shared a platform with Argentina-born evangelist Luis Palau, who addressed an estimated crowd of 700,000 at a rally in Guatemala City.

It was also not surprising that, during Rios Montt's time as president, there was tension between the Protestants and Catholics who were becoming alarmed as more and more of the population were embracing evangelical Christianity. Some estimates say that twenty-five per cent of this once Catholic nation is now Protestant.

Catholic sources, however, claim that eighty-eight per cent of the total population are baptised Catholics. But a recent survey of Protestants has revealed that there are now over 200 established denominations and estimates suggest Protestants exceed twenty per cent of the population. Evangelism has gone on despite the current unrest. Most of this growth has occurred among the *ladino* (Spanish-speaking) population, although several 'people movements' are also occurring in tribal areas.

Because of the strong evangelistic efforts of the Protestants, I heard reports of signs being posted on the doorways of some Catholic homes which said,

'These doors are closed if you are not Catholic. We do not accept any Protestant propaganda.'

The Catholic Church certainly had an historical priority on the allegiance of the Guatemalan people. It had first moved into Guatemala in the sixteenth century in the wake of the Spanish conquest of the area. The *World Christian Encyclopedia*, edited by David B Barrett and published by Oxford University Press, notes that 'From 1524 to 1821, Guatemala was the centre of the Spanish government in Central America, with which the Catholic Church was closely associated. Little change took place after Guatemala's independence. In 1871 the church was separated from the state and its property confiscated; and in 1874 the religious orders were dissolved.'

Today the Catholic Church in Guatemala suffers from a shortage of priests, perhaps because the large number of Indians who are Catholic have little interest in the priesthood. For them, baptism is in fact the only sacrament widely accepted, although there is a high level of lay participation in the ceremonial aspects of village religious life.

Protestantism (American-style) entered Guatemala in 1882 when missionaries were invited in by President Barrios, who felt that Protestants could make a contribution to the progress and development of the country. The Presbyterians were the first to respond and now the National Presbyterian Church of Guatemala, which became fully autonomous in 1962, is one of the largest of the traditional non-Pentecostal Protestant churches.

Following on the heels of the Presbyterians were missionaries from the Central American Mission, who arrived in 1899. Autonomous since 1927, its Robinson Bible Institute has been preparing pastors for work among Indians since 1923, and another Bible institute in Guatemala City trains leaders for all Central American countries.

As is true in most Latin American countries, Pentecostals, although beginning much later—about 1916 in Guatemala—have shown the largest growth. Guatemala's largest single Protestant denomination is the Assemblies of God which began in 1937.

There are also indigenous churches that have been formed in Guatemala. This is a recent phenomenon, and the majority of these independent churches are Pentecostal, the largest of which is the Church of the Prince of Peace.

Formed in 1956 by Jose Maria Munoz, many of the original members of the Prince of Peace movement had transferred from various Assemblies of God congregations. The new churches began to spread quickly. One of the main reasons for the rapid growth was a daily thirty-minute radio message directed to pastors, teachers and lay leaders in remote areas where limited resources were available. By 1974, there were fourteen radio programmes in Guatemala, Mexico, Honduras, El Salvador and Nicaragua. By 1979, there were 518 churches with 33,670 members.

The Elim Christian Mission is another fast-growing denomination in Central America. It began as a small house church in Guatemala City in 1961. One of the first members of this group, Dr. Otoniel Rios, a well-known medical doctor, was responsible for the development of a large central church in Guatemala City and began a radio ministry in 1970 which became very popular and attracted many to the church. By 1981, the total membership exceeded 15,000 and the Elim Christian Mission continued to grow as fast as any denomination in Central America.

Both Catholics and Protestants have been very much involved in education and social service. The presbyterian church sponsors six secondary schools, five clinics, a cultural and recreational centre, and an agricultural extension programme. The Protestants also have, in addition, their own university, Universidad Mariano Galvez, the first of its kind to be established in Latin America. It was opened in 1966.

Now that Rios Montt is out of power—he was overthrown on August 8, 1983, by forces led by his own defence minister, General Oscar Mejia Victores—there are fears that sectarian violence could really erupt in the country. After seizing power in the coup that some believe was supported by the Pentagon in Washington, D.C., General Victores launched a stinging attack on Rios Montt and the Verbo Church as a 'fanatical and aggressive' religious group.

In fact, a backlash against Evangelicals did take place shortly after Montt was removed from power. On August 12, 1983, a rock-throwing group forced and partly destroyed the door of the Latin American Library in Guatemala City which belongs to the Cutural Association of Latin America, an evangelical organisation, in an attempt to burn down the building. Four days later, various inspectors from the Ministry of Public Education arrived at the Evangelical Institute of Latin America, which belongs to the same group as the Library, to investigate their academic programme and to find out if the students were 'obligated to take religion classes in the Institute'.

The Elim Church of Guatemala City received an anonymous threat that a bomb would explode during its evening service. After discussion, the church decided not to close but to hold the evening service one hour early. More than 8,000 people attended Sunday services in its warehouse-like central church, on the western outskirts of the capital.

Ricardo Gonzalez, at the time head of Open Doors research in Latin America, told me, 'The tension that now exists between Catholics and Evangelicals in Guatemala is being fully reported and debated in the press and on television'. Evangelical leaders want very much to show the apolitical character of their churches in order to avoid further misunderstandings with the new government or the Catholic Church.

In a 1984 interview with the newspaper *Prensa Libre*, Archbishop Prospero Penados del Barrio, the country's Roman Catholic prelate, was quoted as saying that the evangelical groups were spreading 'hatred' in their efforts to expand. He reportedly blamed U.S. influences, since many of the groups have ties to U.S. church organisations.

'That it (the evangelical movement) is growing at an unprecedented rate is certainly the case,' said William D Taylor, director of post-graduate studies at the Central American Theological Seminary, which is affiliated with CAM International, one of the traditional Protestant missionary organisations.

According to Dr. Taylor, an estimated 1.6 million of Guatemala's nearly 8 million population are evangelical Christians, up from 308,000 in 1967. (Some say there are even more than this figure.) There are at least 8,000 evangelical churches in the country.

Journalist Ron Howell, in an article for the *Associated Press*, gave his personal insight into the evangelical boom in the country: 'Several evangelical leaders who were interviewed said converts are looking for something new that will add a feeling of stability in their lives.

'Others say the fundamentalist trend indicates a dissatisfaction with the Catholic Church, which they say has become complacent during its centuries of religious predominance in the region.

'They also note that Evangelicals seem constantly at work, creating youth programmes and women's groups, and proselytising on television and the radio.'

Fortunately, this tension has apparently eased for the moment, and Evangelicals have continued their 'Experiment in Righteousness'. Evangelicals broadcast 100 radio programmes a day throughout the country and own five radio stations.

A new newspaper, *La Palabra* (The Word), with a circulation of 6,000—out of total daily circulation in the whole country of 100,000—has passed three rivals to gain third place in national sales. The newspaper, under its director and managing editors, Rafael Escorbar Arguello (who was President Rios Montt's assistant press secretary), carries international, national, and local news and sports, along with a 'Christian Section' that includes coverage of church-related events, testimonies, devotional thoughts, and articles on topics of current religious interest.

Now the Catholics have decided to take action to counter the Protestants. 'The church is creating various programmes and trying to become more active,' reported Julio Santos, editor of the *Prensa Libre* section that published the controversial interview with the archbishop. 'It wants to conquer the ground that it has lost'.

I returned to Guatemala in March, 1984 to interview Efrain Rios Montt. With me were Dr. Ben Armstrong, Executive Director of the American-based National Religious Broadcasters, and photojournalist, Kate Rafferty. I was able to persuade the ex-president to break his self-imposed silence.

He told me of a recent trip he had made to Puebla, Mexico, where he spoke at a church conference.

'I begged them to do whatever they could to send pastors here. And in that way they won't have to send in the Marines,' he told me in the Church of the Word School in Guatemala City, where he was Vice principal.

'I believe the only way to change Latin America is to know Christ.' He agreed that the only answer for his terror-torn region was 'in the Bible, not in bullets'.

If anyone can speak with authority on this, it is Efrain Rios Montt. Maybe, if Guatemala heeds his words, his unique 'Experiment in Righteousness' will not have been in vain.

I will leave the last word on Guatemala, however, to Dr. Peter Wagner, Professor of Church Growth at Fuller Seminary's School of World Missions in Pasadena, California, who told a gathering of 400 pastors, missionaries and key lay leaders in Antigua, Guatemala, in May 1984, 'Along with Korea, China, Ethiopia, Indonesia and the Philippines, Guatemala is a flash point in the growth of the church worldwide'.

The question still to be answered is, 'Will that "flash point" lead Guatemala's Christians to become much more involved in justice and peace for their country?' If not, the 'flash point' they will experience will almost certainly be a bloody one!

4: Passing through the fire

By J. W. Meyer

With the triumph of the Sandinista revolution in mid-1979, Central America reached a boiling point of revolutionary activity. A state of political uncertainty and outright civil disorder spread beyond Nicaragua's borders as the Sandinistas, who take their name from pre-World War II revolutionary hero Augusto Sandino, were welcomed by the great majority of Nicaraguans and were cheered throughout the Americas by people from all levels of society who had joined in the crusade to end Anastasio Somoza's tyrannical dictatorship.

For three generations the Somoza family ruled Nicaragua as though the country were a private family holding, allowing limited civil liberties as long as they did not interfere with the aims and goals of the Somoza political machine.

As the FSLN (Sandinista Front for National Liberation) gained popularity and momentum in the late 1970s, both clergy and laity, in the Catholic and Protestant sectors, welcomed the idea of a pluralistic decentralised democratic system promised by the Sandinistas. The middle class, also weary of Somoza's iron grip over the economy, had eventually supported the Sandinista revolution wholeheartedly. The support of the business sector effectively contributed

45

to the downfall of the dictatorship.

But the advent of Sandinista rule did not immediately usher in the long-awaited democracy. As the new rulers made clear, their Marxist oriented ideology and delayed steps toward a democratic system. Although the press suffered from limited censorship under the Somozas, the nation soon discovered how arbitrary censorship can be under today's Sandinista regime.

In January 1985, the former editor of the country's only independent newspaper, Pedro Joaquin Chamorro, stated that the Nicaraguan press now suffers from the most severe censorship ever enforced in the history of Latin America. An often-heard statement on city buses, 'Before we had one dictator, now we have nine,' expressed the acute disappointment felt by many Nicaraguans.

The nine-member *junta*, which ruled Nicaragua until the November 1984 election, made several moves which impacted the Church: first, by purging the largely Protestant Miskito Indian nation in a violent attempt to relocate the entire tribe far from its native homeland; second, by carrying out a massive ideological indoctrination campaign as a part of a national literacy campaign [some Nicaraguans believe that the ultimate aim of the literacy campaign was to consolidate Sandinista control over the entire population, because it seemed to be a part of introducing the Cuban-styled CDS (Sandinistian Committee of Defence) block committee programme]; and third, by attempting to establish a controlling grip over the Church, both Catholic and Protestant.

In early 1980, neither clergy nor laity had a clear notion of the probable aims of the Sandinistas regarding Church affairs. A group of 700 pastors met at that time with the junta and offered their unconditional support to the new government. Yet, by the end of that year the revolutionary government had asked all foreign missionaries to leave the country and began pressuring denominations with U.S. ties to sever them because these were, according to the Sandinistas, 'just another element at the forefront of imperialistic expansion and aggression'.

In 1981, the situation of the Protestant church reached a low ebb. While Nicaraguans had begun to realise that the Sandinistas were not installing the promised democracy, they did not expect any sudden interference in Church affairs. But the Sandinistas seemed to be using tactics that would divide and eventually break the Church.

According to former Sandinista state security agent Miguel Bolaños, the Sandinistas viewed the Church as a threat to their total domination over the Nicaraguan people, and had developed elaborate plans to divide the Church. Of his discussions with pro-Marxist priests participating in the revolutionary process, Bolaños confessed:

We would talk about how religious ideas should be used with Christians who were working with us as security agents: for example, some of the La Salle brothers believed in liberation theology, but for us, the Sandinistas, we didn't believe in any theology. It was only a matter of using it in the revolutionary process to divide the church.

And while we used these priests and their liberation theology for this purpose, we also realised that in the future it could be a threat to us. That is why we had to recruit a lot of priests that were leaders in this line of thought, to compromise them and ensure their future loyalty.

We were even thinking of introducing Sandinista young people into seminary to become priests. They would have to sacrifice themselves 10 to 15 years to become Catholic priests, but would be Sandinistas in the future. We were thinking about that because we were already doing it in other churches, such as the evangelical churches, where it was easier to become a minister. We (state security) had young evangelical people that were not in the ministry at the moment, but they would be in six months or a year, with good direction.*

The first religious groups to feel the impact of the Sandinista suppression were the Jehovah's Witnesses, the Seventh Day Adventists, and the Mormon Church, whose churches were confiscated during April and May of 1982. Evangelical churches in rural areas, far from the scrutiny of the international press, did not fare much better. Many churches were burned and others confiscated temporarily for military use, especially in the conflict areas. Church members became terrorised and many pastors fled the country. In the most extreme cases, Christians resorted to an underground existence for the sake of survival.

Practically all of the rural churches which were confiscated at that time have since been returned, but many of them were so desecrated by Sandinista troops that Christians refused to hold worship services in them again.

It was during this period that both the Catholic and Protestant church leadership began feeling pressure to participate in the government-endorsed Popular

*'The Subversion of the Church in Nicaragua: An interview with Miguel Bonaños Hunter.' (Washington: The Institute on Religion and Democracy, December 1983.)

Church. As a Marxist–Leninist state, the Sandinistas sought the absorption of the Church by the state, and this they hoped to accomplish through the Popular Church.

Knowing Latin culture is to know that it is deeply religious and loyal to the Catholic Church of Rome. In order to create a godless society one must first find a way to persuade the masses that the new politics are not godless. An interesting phrase made possible by liberation theology, zealously embraced in Nicaragua today, is 'Marxist Christian'.

'In the mountains we were given a view of religion that blurred the differences between Christianity and Marxism,' said former agent Miguel Bolaños.

The Popular Church has developed into a sophisticated blend of liberation theology and the ideologies of Marx, Engels and Lenin. But, because many churches have not allowed Marxist ideology or liberation theology to creep into the Sunday morning sermons, they have unfortunately suffered attacks from *turbas divinas*. Believed to be organised by state security and comprised of members of the local CDS committees, these well trained terrorist mobs are feared particularly for their violent attacks on unsuspecting churches, or otherwise identified anti-Sandinista meetings. Eyewitness testimonies indicate that their intent is to terrorise by clubbing innocent victims, smashing private property and disrupting the meetings at whatever cost.

Christians confess that 1983 and 1984 were their most difficult years. Although the Sandinistas ceased to confiscate churches and the outright violence against Christians was tempered, (because this tactic proved ineffective in incorporating the vast majority of Evangelicals into the political system,) they had introduced a more subtle approach. Telephone poles, whitewashed walls, and office buildings were plastered with graffiti glorifying the revolution and vilifying those who were perceived to be enemies of it.

SANDINO YESTERDAY, TODAY AND FOR-EVER, and KARL MARX LIVES AND TRANS-FORMS THE WORLD, confused Christian thought with political rhetoric. Painted on the outside walls of the homes of many Christians considered unsympathetic to the revolutionary cause appeared crudely painted threats: CAREFUL! WE'RE WATCHING YOU. PHARISEE. SOMOCISTA. HERE LIVES A THEOLOGIAN OF DEATH. CONTRA.

With these messages, the Sandinistas identified Christians as traitors and enemies of the revolution. This psychological pressure has at times seemed unbearable. During the early years of the revolution, Christians had been able to hide in their homes and churches, even though they lived in constant fear of the turbas. Now they were exposed to their neighbours' hate.

A quick review of the state of church affairs by national denominational leaders revealed a church in retreat, divided and demoralised. The Evangelical Committee for Relief and Development (CEPAD), founded in 1972 to aid earthquake victims, noting the unstable condition of the Church in post-revolutionary Nicaragua, formed a sub-committee uniting all evangelical pastors under one banner.

(Although CEPAD maintained a neutral position during the Somoza years, it gave its full endorsement to the Sandinistas when they came to power. Today CEPAD is recognised by the revolutionary government as the sole voice of the evangelical church.)

The new National Council of Evangelical Pastors

(CNPEN) was welcomed as an organisation that could unite the churches and the first elected executive committee was comprised of many prominent denominational leaders, including those from the Assemblies of God and the Baptist Convention. But, within one year of its inception, CNPEN felt it had to separate itself from CEPAD; first, because of the latter's increasing political role in the Sandinista government; and second, because of CEPAD's questionable management of foreign aid funds.

With this separation, CNPEN gained greater esteem within the national evangelical Church, while hostility and distrust toward CEPAD increased. Acting independently of CEPAD, the National Council leaders sought to unite the Church and breathe new life into it. Leaders encouraged Christians to be bold instead of hiding in their churches; and to view Nicaragua as a field to be won for Christ, rather than a war-torn country from which to flee.

Acting with a sort of blind confidence in God, the National Council voted to stage a week-long crusade in Managua during January 1984. Although there was no reason to believe that the Sandinistas would approve the use of a public arena in which to hold the event, organisers went ahead with their plans. It was an experiment, because Christians were well aware of the fact that no such crusades had taken place in their country since before the triumph of the revolution. The Campus Crusade staff trained one thousand counsellors, and young people from many surrounding cities carried out a word-of-mouth campaign on buses, in theatres, and in public areas, inviting the public to the crusade.

Although organisers realised that the odds were against them on every count, Christians seemed supernaturally inspired and determined to see the crusade through to the end. The tiny Christian radio station, Ondas de Luz, became the sole media promoter of the event when the Sandinistas prohibited crusade advertisements and notices to be placed in newspapers, secular radio, and on television.

Organisers met privately with government representatives, asking for the assignment of a suitable meeting place, but each request was met with a firm denial. In desperation, the thousand-plus counsellors met at Managua's 12,000-seat bullring, a possible location, and formed a prayer ring around it, claiming victory over the government's decision.

The organisers returned optimistically to meet with government representatives, but the continued denials had begun to wear on the Christian leaders. When the invited evangelist, Alberto Mottesi, arrived, organisers met him with discouragement in their hearts. Yet, Mottesi's strong confrontive nature renewed their hope and a visit to Sandinista offices with him seemed to rekindle the spirit of victory among the Nicaraguan Christians.

Not until 4.00 p.m. of the day the crusade was scheduled to begin did word arrive from the government that permission was granted to hold the meetings in the Catholic University's 50,000-seat baseball stadium. The city immediately took on a festive air. Vendors pushed their carts into place around the outer ring of the structure and the many organising committees and sub-committees scurried around setting up lights and sound, putting in place security precautions and, above all, getting out the word of the location. Incredible as it seems, three hours later the crusade began with over 10,000 in attendance. By the end of the week, the count each evening was well over 50,000.

In retrospect, leaders believe that the eleventh-hour permission to stage the event was designed to embarrass the Christians. Although their request had been for the use of a bullring seating only 12,000, the government gave them the baseball stadium with space for over 50,000, possibly hoping that a poor opening turnout would only be more conspicuous in a larger facility, and thus prove a pre-supposed disinterest in the Gospel in post-revolutionary Nicaragua.

This was not the case. Each night Christians filled the stadium to overflowing and sang hymns and choruses that could be heard even at a great distance. Each night organisers battled the threat of turbas, the presence of state security agents, the mischievous pranks by the Sandinista Youth (like Russia's Young Pioneers), but these unfortunate mini-episodes could not mar the triumph of the crusade.

Perhaps for the first time since the revolution, Christians shed their fear and openly cried with joy each night as Mottesi preached the Gospel with power and conviction. His most memorable statement drew a hush from the crowd as he pointed out, 'You think you have the answer to the world's problems. But I tell you that Moscow doesn't have the answer! Havana doesn't have the answer! Washington doesn't have the answer! Jesus Christ is the only one who can change your life and give you freedom!'

The following night, the government ordered the power to be cut off in the section of the city where the crusade was being held. Also, bus routes were detoured so crusade goers were forced to walk several kilometres out of their way in order to reach the stadium. But it made no difference. Christians were ready to make a statement and the awful blanket of fear had ceased to dominate them.

As one church leader later expressed it, 'The Church is not afraid any longer; instead, we're coming up for air.' Christians have pushed through the doors of their churches and streamed out onto the city streets with the Gospel. The director of Nicaragua's Campus Crusade office claimed that by early 1985 the entire country had been exposed to the Gospel at least twice due to outreach efforts that stemmed from the great crusade.

The battle for the control of the ideology of Nicaraguans is not over yet. Relative freedom exists, more so in the cities nearest Managua, where the international press is active, than in the rural areas where foreign visitors are rare.

Ration coupons are a way of life, but many Christian families still refuse to apply for them in spite of increased shortages of all basic necessities. As the CDS committees consolidate their power and position within the Nicaraguan infrastructure, citizens are becoming more and more dependent on them for even the most basic food products. Yet, before receiving the ration card, citizens are asked to sign a statement acknowledging that the only solution to Nicaragua's problems is the Sandinista revolution. Many Christians balk when confronted with this requirement and have opted to go without rather than sign.

Since the November 1984 presidential election, the Church has continued to grow and bear much fruit. Today, the entire northern region of Nicaragua is experiencing an unprecedented revival which is accompanied by signs and wonders that have sent shock waves throughout the rural communities. The northern provinces of Matagalpa, Chinandega, and Nueva Segovia have been ravaged by the war between the Sandinistas and rebel forces. While many civilians have fled the most affected areas, the Christian community has chosen to stay and bear witness to God's faithfulness and protection over His people.

'In the mountains, the Christians are the only ones who are in high spirits,' says a church leader. 'We are in the hour of God. Soldiers come in (to the churches) with rifles and after accepting Christ they go back and preach to their friends. Soldiers are asking for Bibles because the Christians have made such an impact on them.'

One pastor in Matagalpa could hardly contain his joy when asked about the revival in his region. 'In our church *all* the gifts of the Spirit are manifested!'

Of all the miracles that have occurred in recent months, the most spectacular are those that have demonstrated God's love for His people by protecting them in dangerous situations. Christians point to the fact that churches directly in the line of battle have never suffered damage while Christians have been inside. Bombs either explode in the air over the churches, or they fall into the ground nearby and do not explode.

In one instance, fighting broke out in the outskirts of Paloblan. Immediately the brethren raced to the church to pray. One believer arrived late, but he felt strongly that, in this case, they should instead go to his home to pray. The believers agreed, and as they hurried down the street a bomb fell on the church and blew it to bits.

In another incident, a Christian farmer and his family were caught in the midst of heavy cross-fire between the rebels and government forces. As they attempted to escape the gunfire, they realised that they were surrounded on all sides. Their wooden plank shack offered little protection but they quickly gathered inside, lay flat against the cold dirt floor and began to pray for God's protection.

Although terrifying explosions rocked the house and screams of agony filled the air, they never once stopped praying and trusting in God for their survival. They could hear trees splitting from the heavy mortar blasts and machine-gun fire slamming into the boards of their home. They reported they were afraid to even open their eyes as the battle raged on.

Gradually the fighting stopped and both sides began to retreat; the noises and rumblings moved farther and farther away. Carefully the family got up and began to survey the damage. Outside, the destruction was indescribable. Trees lying in splinters, twisted and useless from repeated impacts, left the family speechless. They stared at the house in great wonder, as they realised that not a single bullet or projectile had passed through the thin walls. Yet all around the house they saw a mass of bullets 'spread out like sand,' proving that God had placed a shield around them and saved their lives.

'We want to record all these testimonies so that the whole world will know what is happening here,' said a twenty-three-year-old pastor. 'We don't ever want to forget the miracles we have seen and heard about.'

Nicaraguan leaders recognise that there are many lessons they can learn from Christians who have suffered even greater hardship than the Nicaraguan Church. Nicaraguan leaders feel that a real threat still lies ahead of them. One leader voiced this in an unforgettable request made in late 1984: 'Please send someone who can teach us how to establish the underground Church. But we don't want to teach this to those of us who are leaders now. Teach this to those who will lead the Church after we're gone.'

5: The bell: safe haven in Honduras

By Dan Wooding

'Save the bell, save the bell,' screamed the distraught Miskito women as the whooping and yelling Sandinista soldiers torched their church.

As the fire took hold on their Moravian sanctuary, men from the Nicaraguan village close to the Honduran border dashed into the blazing church and clambered up the bell tower. Despite the choking smoke and flames, they were able to loosen the precious bell and drop it down to safety.

As the Miskito men dragged the venerable old bell away from the devastation, the bell tower that had housed it crashed unceremoniously to the ground.

By now every house in their village was ablaze. Years of possessions had been destroyed; their Bibles and hymnals were charred ruins; cattle lay dead in the streets, shot by the soldiers who were moving on to the next village for another 'scorched earth' campaign of terror against these peace-loving Indians.

'We carried the bell the eleven miles to the Honduras border, got it across the river, and then a further thirty miles to this refugee camp,' related a Miskito woman in Mocoron Camp, a refugee centre administered by World Relief, under the supervision of the United Nations High Commission on Refugees.

Now that very bell is being used to call the mainly evangelical Miskitos to worship. It is a defiant symbol of their courage and faith in the face of great persecution.

These Miskito Indian refugees joined thousands of other refugees that have flooded into Honduras, a seemingly safe corner in a troubled part of the world. Probably the least progressive of the Central American countries, and the poorest, this one nation has also received refugees from Guatemala, El Salvador and Nicaragua (in addition to the Miskito Indians).

Well over 25,000 Salvadoran refugees have crossed the border into Honduras. Because of the dangers along that border, they have been scattered in villages throughout the country.

These refugees were fleeing suppression and war in El Salvador, but have been greeted with suspicion and apprehension in Honduras. Discrimination against Salvadorans is common because of the past conflicts arising from constant movement from densely populated El Salvador, which seemingly must export some of its people even in times of peace.

Both the Guatemalan and Salvadoran refugees are very much like the Honduran peasants, and they can fade into rural living patterns easily. The Miskito Indians present different problems, because they are actively fighting for cultural survival. At the same time, they are caught in international pressures over which they have no control.

In 1957, a long-quiet border dispute between Nicaragua and Honduras had erupted again. It was precisely the thinly-populated area to the west of the Coco River that was involved; the area in Honduras occupied by a part of the Miskito nation.

This disputed territory had been awarded to Honduras after international mediation by Alphonso XIII of Spain in 1906. But when Honduras began to build roads into it, and allowed foreign companies to explore for oil, Nicaragua reasserted its claims.

Immediately after the Sandinista victory in Nicaragua, some of the *comandantes* began to talk about territories they wanted to reclaim. One area mentioned was the Guanacaste province of Costa Rica. Another, the Coco River territory.

Of course, the people in the way were the Miskito Indians, who were already resisting the changes the revolutionary government wanted to introduce. Their story is of immediate interest to us, because more than 60 per cent of these people are Protestants, primarily Moravians.

The Sandinista government arrested, during 1981, some 253 Moravian leaders, including 109 Moravian pastors and 140 elders. They also imprisoned many of the village and tribal leaders of this traditionally peaceful and industrious tribe. Some were eventually released but at least 130 were sentenced to prison for terms ranging up to 20 years for their alleged part in a conspiracy that was dubbed the 'Red Christmas Plot.'

There are an estimated 125,000 of this outstanding indigenous ethnic group that for centuries has preserved its distinctiveness. The Miskitos inhabit the largely desolate Atlantic Coast region, earning their living mainly as hunters and fishermen. That was until the Sandinistas moved against them. Under the Sandinista rule, the Miskitos have come to experience what one Nicaraguan journalist described as 'the worst cultural dislocation in centuries.'

In the spring of 1984, I flew by MAF (Mission Aviation Fellowship) plane to visit these Miskito Indians (some say the name is derived from 'mosquito', an insect that definitely infests the region they are from). My destination was the Mocoron Camp, which is about 250 miles northeast of Tegucigalpa, the Honduran capital.

Leading our team was the Reverend Tom Claus, a member of the Turtle clan of the Mohawk Tribe from Six Nations Reserve near Brampton, Ontario, and president of CHIEF (Christian Hope Indian Eskimo Fellowship). Claus was making his third visit to the Miskitos. He had already, through Indian Christians in North America, provided them with blankets, lanterns, tools, housing, food, Bibles in the Miskito language, musical instruments and hymnals, but this time he was bearing a communion set large enough to serve 1,000 of these Indians at a time. Also in the group was a Totonac Indian leader from Mexico, Manuel Arenas, who heads up the Totonac Bible Center, and Daniel Lozano, pastor/teacher of the Spanish Department of Grace Community Church in California.

As we stood on the runway beside the airplane, we were surrounded by many smiling men, who took turns in hugging us, and Claus told me why he had brought the communion sets.

'On my last visit to the camp, I asked the Miskitos to tell me the one thing they wanted most,' he said. 'They answered, "We would like to celebrate the Lord's Supper. Could you send us a communion set for at least 1,000 people? We will take turns using it."'

'Even in their desperate need for clothes, food and shelter, their first thought was worship and devotion to their Heavenly Father. I was touched by their sincere desire to fellowship in God's presence.'

Claus was near to tears when, the day after our arrival, Pastor Nabut Zacharias, a Moravian minister, called his believers together for their first communion service since they had fled Nicaragua some two years previously.

He chose a spot on the banks of the fast-flowing Mocoron River and his flock turned over their dugout canoes to use them as pews. Old and young alike solemnly remembered the Lord's Supper against the backdrop of jungle river-life.

Then Claus told the Miskitos, 'I am an Indian and so your pain is my pain; your suffering is my suffering, and I want my people in the United States and Canada to help bear your burden at this time.

'But more than that, Jesus is bearing your burden and He is representing you before the Father. You are not deserted; you are not alone before the Father. You can know you are not deserted and alone because we Christians of North America want to stand with you, and we know God is with you.

'In your suffering we want you to know that there are many of us who care, so cast your cares on us, and on the Lord, for we care deeply for you.'

Suffering is something these Indians certainly know all about. And as I listened to them recount their many horror stories, I could understand why U.S. Ambassador to the United Nations, Jeane J Kirkpatrick, has compared the Sandinista's treatment of them with Adolf Hitler's atrocities against the Jews.

One of the worst of these atrocities took place in December 1981, in the village of Cruce de las Balsas. This village was just one of many in the zone the Sandinistas, anxious to strengthen their borders, had designated as a 120-mile-long 'military zone'. Soldiers began expelling the Indians from their villages and force-marching men and women, the weak, the aged, the young, through the jungles to what Tom Claus described as 'concentration camps' much deeper into the interior to the south.

'The soldiers seemed to come in looking for blood, especially if anyone offered resistance. They buried alive thirty-five of our men,' said one pastor. 'They just left them as we stood helplessly by until they had suffocated and died.'

There was one survivor, a teenager, who managed to claw his way out of the covered-in hole. As he staggered away, he was shot at by a soldier and hit in the arm. He was in the Mocoron Camp when I visited there, but with only one arm.

A Miskito mother described the scene when she and her family tried to cross the Coco River which divides Nicaragua and Honduras.

'We were paddling our dugout canoe across the river when the soldiers took aim at us,' the mother related, her eyes still conveying the horror of that time. 'I let out a scream as my little girl was shot, then my husband. Two more of my children were also hit by the soldiers' bullets.'

Within seconds, four members of this Christian Miskito family fleeing their homeland had been murdered. Their boat sank and the mother, clutching her remaining child, managed to swim to the bank. She watched as the bullet-riddled bodies of the others floated down the river and out to sea.

Much of the travail of the Miskito Indians documented by Humberto Belli is in his book, *Christians Under Fire* (San Jose, Costa Rica: Instituto Puebla, 1984). Belli is a Nicaraguan who left his country in April 1982 in order to speak and write about the experience of Christians in Nicaragua and to draw attention to Marxist manipulation of the Church in Latin America.

Belli was a Marxist and a collaborator with the Sandinistas who became a convert to Christianity in 1977. After the victory of the revolution in 1979, he became the editorial-page editor of the independent newspaper, *La Prensa*, and dealt frequently with church/state issues. According to Belli, the imposition of total censorship in March, 1982 made his work impossible and he decided to carry on abroad.

Belli describes how the Sandinistas used 'revolutionary Christians' to divide and weaken the churches of the country. This enabled them to move directly and aggressively against some of the non-revolutionary religious organisations.

'The first Christians to experience direct government hostility were the Moravian missionaries based in the isolated Atlantic region, the area where the Miskitos and other Indian minorities live,' he said. 'During more than a century of missionary effort the Moravians had provided the Miskitos with the bulk of their churches, schools, and hospitals. Shortly after the triumph of the revolution, however, the Sandinistas began to persecute the Moravian missionaries in order to replace their leadership and influence with that of Sandinista militants, many of them Cubans. In the wake of the unrest that such action stirred among the Miskitos, the Sandinistas gaoled several Moravian missionaries and killed some of them, alleging that they were inciting the Miskitos to rebel against the authorities and that they were CIA agents.'

An authoritative witness to what was happening was a University of California–Berkeley professor, Bernard Nietschmann, who spent two and a half months with the Miskitos in 1983. He gave the following report about the denial of religious freedom to the Miskitos:

'Only in those villages now under the protection of Miskito warriors (anti-Sandinista rebels) are religious services being held. For some villages I visited, that protection had only recently been secured. And even in this large zone many villages cannot hold church services because their religious leaders are in jail or are in exile in Honduras or Costa Rica.

'During the Sandinista military occupation of villages, churches have commonly been used as jails, to detain men and women accused or suspected of counter-revolutionary activities. Churches have also been used to house the Sandinista soldiers. Bibles and hymnbooks have been destroyed. Villagers accuse the Sandinista soldiers of defecating and urinating in the churches. There are many credible reports of these activities. I heard reports of churches that had been burned elsewhere in Indian communities, but in the areas I visited I saw no churches that had been destroyed.

'The Miskitos are a very religious people, and they have suffered greatly from the denial of their freedom of religion. In almost all of my discussions with hundreds of Miskito men and women, this was a principal grievance they reported to me.'

Belli believes that a 'lack of anthropological sensitivity' could be a reason for the events that have taken place. 'But by itself insensitivity could by no means precipitate the chain of events that has disrupted the Miskitos' entire way of life,' he said. 'It took something much greater than mere ignorance and insensitivity to so deeply upset the Miskitos as to produce a massive exodus and turn peaceful fishermen into guerrilla fighters.'

Belli says that the tensions surfaced shortly after the Sandinistas' victory in July 1979. He believes the victors did not acknowledge the 'traditional network of indigenous leadership and authority—including the Elders Council, representative of 256 communities, by which the Miskitos have governed themselves.' He states that instead the Sandinistas tried to destroy the Miskitos' local system of government and replace the Indian authorities with Sandinista Defense Committees, made up mostly of Sandinista militants from the pacific region.

He continues: 'Starting in 1979, the Sandinistas began to replace the Miskitos' centuries-old tradition of communal ownership of farmland by a system of state-operated farms. Land which had been claimed and used by Miskito communities was declared state-owned. In addition, the state barred the Indians from cutting the wood in such areas.

'These policies alienated the Indian population and caused widespread unrest. The Sandinistas responded ruthlessly. They accused their critics of being counter-revolutionaries, stormed the headquarters of several Indian organisations and Moravian offices and churches, made mass arrests, and killed some Miskito leaders. One of these was Lyster Athders, prominent leader and member of the Elders Council, who disappeared during imprisonment in September, 1979. His body was never found.'

It was not surprising that the Miskitos began a series of mass demonstrations against the Sandinistas. One action that really angered the Miskitos was when, in 1980, foreign teachers, especially Cubans, took over many of the Moravian schools. 'The Sandinistas forced the inclusion of three chapters on Marxist–Leninist theory in the educational materials of the Miskitos' literacy campaign,' says Belli.

He affirms that the brutal actions of the Sandinistas caused some of the Miskitos—'a very peaceful people who can be drawn into fighting only under extreme provocation'—to take up arms in 1982.

In October, 1983, Bernard Nietschmann, who is also consultant to the human rights commission of the Organisation of American States, gave a sweeping description of the Sandinistas mistreatment of the Miskitos. Nietschmann, who many believe to be the world's leading outside authority on the Miskito Indians, said after his two and a half months inside their territories that he had found 'widespread, systematic and arbitrary human rights violations by the Sandinista government, including arbitrary killings, arrests and interrogations; rapes; torture; continuing forced relocations of village populations; destruction of villages; restriction and prohibition of freedom of travel; prohibition of village food production; restriction and denial of any access to basic and necessary store foods; the complete absence of any medicine, health care, or educational services in many villages; the denial of religious freedom; and the looting of households and sacking of villages.'

Belli has his own view of why this has all taken place. 'The Miskito tragedy can be traced to the earliest days after the success of the revolution, when most other governments were still on friendly terms with the Sandinista regime,' he says. 'Thus, the government's treatment of the Miskitos did not stem from a need to combat outside pressures. If a single causal factor for the Miskito's tribulation is to be identified, it is the Sandinistas' determination to reshape Nicaraguan society according to a Marxist model: an intention which violated deeply-rooted

Miskito traditions and aspirations. The Miskitos have not been incorrect in perceiving the Sandinistas as a fundamental threat to their traditional way of life and beliefs, for so the Sandinistas are.

'Mass relocations of entire populations and the obliteration of indigenous cultures have been a constant in Marxist practice around the world: Stalin "resettled" the kulaks in the twenties and thirties, the Cambodian Reds "resettled" their entire urban population in the seventies. Communism embodies one of the greatest drives toward enforced uniformity found in history. It refashions all social patterns according to a single scheme, and it is not deterred by humanitarian considerations. From a Marxist standpoint, the destruction of those who obstruct the way to utopia means very little. The tragedy of the Miskito is but the most recent in a long series of Communist suppressions of ethnic minorities.'

While I was in Mocoron I was told that the Miskitos are continuing to head for the safety of Honduras from their traditional homeland in the rain forests and swamps along Nicaragua's Caribbean coast, despite the dangers on their escape route, compared by some to the original 'Trail of Tears' along which the Cherokee, Creek and Seminoles were moved from the southeastern part of the United States to the State of Oklahoma about 150 years ago.

Some 25,000 Miskitos have now crossed into Honduras. Included in that number are 1,000 refugees who succeeded in crossing the border on December 24, 1983, after an exhausting march of three days and nights during which they were machine-gunned and bombarded by the Sandinista army.

Pablo Smith, an 81-year-old man with gnarled hands

and a leathery face, and with some of his forty grandchildren gathered around him, told me their incredible escape story in his Caribbean English, a legacy of British control of the Miskito coast in the last century. It seems that Pablo was something of a Pied Piper in helping to lead this dash for freedom.

'We had a total of ninety children, forty of them my own grandchildren, when we began our escape from Nicaragua,' said Pablo, with an accent not unlike that of Jamaicans.

'As we set off, we could see our villages burning. They were all destroyed. Nothing was left. They killed our pigs and cattle. The soldiers just sprayed them with machine-gun fire after burning down our homes.

'For the first few hours we walked up to our waists in mud. It was terrible. Some of the women were suckling their babes and would be so weak they would fall over into the mud.

'Finally, we came to the Savanah, an old Indian trail, and it was much easier. It took us a total of three days and nights to get here to Mocoron. We are grateful to God that we are here and we believe God will continue to help us.'

The first thing they did when they arrived was not to construct homes, but to pitch in and build a church so they could worship together again.

The Miskitos were first evangelised by Moravian missionaries from Europe in the nineteenth century. They have a heritage of evangelical belief.

'Partly for that reason, but also because of differences in language and race, the Nicaraguan government considers them a block to the progress of social reforms' said Dr. Dale W Kietzman, an anthropologist and CHIEF board member.

70

Dr. Kietzman noted that the Miskito Indians were now coming across the border from much further inland than earlier groups who fled into Honduras. 'The situation for the young Miskitos is especially desperate. They have left because they do not feel they will have any chance for a proper education or gainful employment in Nicaragua,' he added.

'Being labelled as "counter-revolutionary" is only the latest in a long history of discrimination against these Indian Christians by their Spanish-speaking countrymen, but it certainly does not shake their Christian faith.'

Tim Goble, president of CA International, a California-based ministry providing spiritual and material help, told me that the suffering these Indians had undergone had caused a real spiritual wakening among them.

Goble, who had made many visits to Mocoron, the hub of the refugee camps in eastern Honduras, said, 'Of course, many of these refugees are Christians. In fact, they are here because they were unwilling to compromise their Christian faith with the Marxist government in their homeland (Nicaragua). But some of the people's faith back then had grown cold and dry; now they are really getting on fire!'

Goble cites the growing number of early morning prayer meetings as one indicator of spiritual renewal. 'Many of the refugee churches start ringing their chimes (usually a small piece of iron) at 4.00 a.m., calling the people to gather for prayer. This goes on every morning, and the churches are usually packed out.

'The refugee churches are overflowing at their Sunday services. A church I spoke at one Sunday morning was so full they have to ask all the children to leave. One of our team members who spoke English held an impromptu Sunday School class for them. Still there were people standing outside looking in.'

Goble, who has worked with emergency teams of medical volunteers and construction workers in Lebanon and Honduras, told me that CA International is dedicated to encouraging believers who are suffering around the world, assisting them to become self-sustaining in their Christian fellowship within their own cultures.

'For instance, this team of volunteers built a trading post, and added an emergency room to the hospital in Mocoron. Contact with these men is a real blessing to the refugees, as well as an encouragement to the relief workers.

'When we were getting ready to depart, the team came to me and said they wanted to leave all their tools with the church I had spoken in that Sunday morning to help them build a larger place to worship. The pastor accepted the tools with tears in his eyes. You just can't beat that kind of love and encouragement.'

Goble then related an incident that took place when walking back with a Miskito pastor from an early-morning prayer meeting.

'I asked them if they prayed like this when they were in Nicaragua. He shook his head and said, "No . . . if we had, maybe we wouldn't be here now." '

If I needed any further evidence of the deeply-held faith of these Indians, I received it whenever I asked one of the Miskitos how he was. 'Fine, by God's grace,' would be his firm reply. It's the answer all Miskitos give to that question.

Despite all that has happened to them, they are still 'Fine, by God's grace.'

A lesson for us all?

6: A time for commitment

By J. W. Meyer

El Salvador means 'the land of the Saviour'. And it has been blessed by God with warm tropical breezes that blow all year round and caress the lush hills and valleys. El Salvador was once the haven of Spanish settlers and fortune seekers. It had also been the birthplace of the independence movement that broke the chains of Spanish colonial power from 1811–1821. Now it appears to have become the showcase for terrorism and institutionalised violence in the Western Hemisphere.

In the late seventies, Salvadorans had watched the revolution in nearby Nicaragua slowly wear away the will of a dictatorship to resist. Church leaders in El Salvador then firmly stated, 'It will never happen here.' Yet, it did.

When Salvadoran guerrillas first came down from the mountains and engaged the army in combat, few took them seriously.

But when brutally dismembered and tortured corpses appeared in the streets of San Salvador, the nation realised it was in serious trouble. Suddenly one's political leanings became a potential life or death matter.

El Salvador has become a nation filled with internal refugees. Once somnolent churches are now faced with the Christian responsibility of caring for the homeless and the poverty-stricken, even when they hold opposing political views.

By 1978, when the Salvadoran people realised that a full-scale civil war could be upon them, the Catholic Church, under the leadership of Archbishop Oscar Arnulfo Romero, who was eventually assassinated, positioned itself on the side of social justice. Where previous homilies dealt with theological matters, these were now replaced with carefully worded political announcements.

While Salvadorans continued to be deeply divided in their political loyalties, there seemed to be no escape from this political discussion, even in the Catholic Church. Some evangelical leaders feel that while this political tension was not the original cause for a sudden growth of the Church, it certainly had contributed to it. The sudden outbreak of uncontrolled violence, with its nightmare of insecurity and desperation, made for hearts willing to hook onto anything that offered hope.

A change in the relatively complacent attitude of the Protestant Church had to start with the leadership. And this change did come very subtly, as the Spirit began to work through individual lives.

There is the example of one pastor who decided to take a stand. One day, God clearly impressed upon him to reach out in love to the revolutionaries.

'Lord, I can't go to them,' he pleaded. 'They'll kill me!' Yet he knew what God wanted him to do and after wrestling with his conscience all night, he finally surrendered.

The pastor bought 200 New Testaments and, despite the protests of his friends, went off to the backlands to find the guerrillas. His first contact came when two machine guns were jabbed in his back.

'What do you want?' the ragged revolutionaries demanded.

'I've come to share God's love with you,' the pastor replied, knowing how absurd it sounded.

'Don't you know we can kill you?'

'Yes, I know, but take these Bibles first.' The guerrilla thumbed through one of the books, then looked up at the pastor.

'You're crazy,' he growled, 'but I have to admire your courage. You've got five minutes to get out of here.' Hurriedly, the pastor departed, leaving the New Testaments behind for the guerrillas. He had followed God's command.

That same night, more than 100 of his fellow pastors were meeting to decide whether or not to leave the country. They spent all night in prayer and then, inspired by the pastor's glowing testimony, decided to stay. 'Our purpose is to glorify Jesus,' they concluded, 'and whether we live or die, this is where we belong.'

Another event that brought the evangelical church out of a state that one leader described as 'A church that was happy in the church,' was the massive evangelistic campaigns which began in 1978. From 1978 through 1980, the guerrilla insurgency so terrorised the nation that Christians could successfully unite in a 'Clamor Por La Paz'—'Clamour for Peace'.

At that time, the Salvadoran military had launched what they called the 'final offensive' to bring the insurgents to their knees. To Church leaders, this was the pivotal moment for introducing the Gospel as an alternative to the left–right conflict. Campus Crusade for Christ launched its well known 'I Found It' campaign, which mobilised 450 churches and over 15,000 workers in 60 cities simultaneously. The impact of the evangelical outreach on a terrorised Salvadoran nation was more than opportune . . . it was providential.

When Christians again united that same year to stage a massive evangelistic campaign, the colourful Puerto Rican evangelist Jorge Raschke filled San Salvador's soccer stadium, and Christians 'lost their fear', according to Salvadoran pastor Luis Panameño.

Although the fastest-growing denomination in El Salvador is the Assemblies of God, the Prince of Peace Church, among other Pentecostal groups, have seen their churches double and even triple in the last five years.

The Church of God in Santa Tecla, a small town near San Salvador, has at times grown at the rate of fifteen new members each week. The Assemblies of God reports no less than 80,000 new baptisms since the conflict began, and other new denominations have sprouted up as a result of the unprecedented church growth.

'This is not the same church of five years back,' noted a Church of God official. But although the harvest has been great, Central American Mission pastor Luis Bush emphatically states that revival has not yet arrived. Others agree with this view.

'The war has brought us closer to God' said Campus Crusade Director, Adonai Leiva. But other things must be accomplished before the revival is complete. An Assemblies of God spokesman emphasised that the higher social classes and government circles have yet to feel the impact of the revival, but new missions-minded Salvadoran churches have made these groups a priority.

Mission '84, a conference on missions held in San Salvador at mid-year, drew well over a thousand young people from many denominations to discuss the issue of becoming a responsible, missionary-sending church. Five years ago the Salvadoran churches could not have conceived of such a possibility; they were not yet at a stage where one denomination would co-operate with another toward a common goal. Open Doors has invariably found that persecution purifies the Church and encourages its growth. But in the years prior to the current revolutionary upheaval in El Salvador, denominational rivalries formed vast chasms dividing evangelical groups.

At the first signs of civil war, Christians had begun to investigate the need to become unified, recognising that an onslaught of political pressure could otherwise weaken them. They took full advantage of the fact that, while the Catholic Church chose to use political themes in Sunday morning homilies, they could offer an answer to the Salvadoran people who were really searching for an inner peace and spiritual fulfilment that would sustain them in this time of trouble.

And they were right in choosing to preach the Gospel of love. For example, although the Church of God had only 187 churches five years ago, today it boasts 374, not including several new mission outposts in the most remote areas of the country. A once small congregation in San Salvador, the Assemblies of God of Monte Carmelo still boasts only 520 members, but in 1983 alone these 500-plus members engaged in a weekly evangelistic street ministry that evangelised over 100,000 people.

Luis Bush, pastor of the largest Central American Mission church in El Salvador, affirmed that his church saw instant results when they first emphasised personal evangelism and street witnessing. The visit of the Pope in 1982 sparked a renewed spiritual interest in the general populace, and in the succeeding two weeks Bush's church led several hundred Salvadorans to Christ during massive street evangelism.

Although the explosion of Church growth has slowed somewhat, those congregations that added several Sunday services to handle the crowds have not seen significant decline. The Evangelistic Centre of the Assemblies of God in San Salvador continues to be one of the success stories of the wartime revival. The three morning worship services are packed to overflowing and the buoyant spirit continues in spite of a gradual return to normality throughout the country.

Although the period of troubles is not over, the election of President Napoleon Duarte marks a new beginning for the democratic process. Territory once considered 'lost' to the guerrilla insurgents has been regained. Many displaced people, the internal refugees, have returned to their homes, and an air of hopefulness is permeating Salvadoran society once again.

Yet, the scars remain. Christians did not entirely escape the vicious killing fields that resulted from the guerrilla/military confrontation. A pastor on his way to a church in a remote area of El Salvador was surrounded by a hostile band of guerrillas who proceeded to stone him and his colleague when they refused to join their revolutionary effort.

'As we were being stoned, I suddenly received a direct hit square in the back, and you cannot imagine the satisfaction I felt. As the Apostle Paul reminded me, it was like a weight of glory,' recalled the young pastor. 'I thought to myself, as the stones hit us, how wonderful it is to be beaten. The next day we went back and preached to them.'

In another case, the Assemblies of God Church in Bolivar la Montana was bombed during a service, and while everyone escaped unharmed, guerrillas quickly surrounded the church and ordered all of the young men to go with them. Many of these young men have not been heard from since.

Reflecting on more than forty Christians in the Assemblies of God Church alone that have suffered martyrdom since the beginning of the conflict, a young Christian leader courageously responded, 'We know we have to be ready to die for Christ at whatever moment; that's why we do what we can now.'

This young leader certainly has plentiful examples of that kind of dedication. For instance, two young ex-guerrillas from El Salvador were brutally assassinated in separate incidents shortly after making commitments to Jesus Christ.

Although the cases seemed unrelated, both Monchini Sanchez and Juan Carlos Mejivares had refused to denounce their new-found faith following persistent threats on their lives. Both were eliminated in carefully planned ambushes before witnesses and friends.

Juan Carlos had chosen at first to remain with the guerrilla forces in order to witness to his comrades. But it wasn't long before he was discovered praying on his knees as he did night guard duty. His life in danger, he fled to Guatemala where he joined an evangelistic film ministry and travelled throughout the country presenting its films.

One evening as he and his co-workers returned to Guatemala City, his former comrades overtook the vehicle and forced it off the road. They ordered Juan Carlos out of the car and, with his friends watching, pumped bullets into his body. He died instantly.

Monchini, once a guerrilla leader specialising in manufacturing bombs and in terrorism, was shopping at a local outdoor market in Usulutan, where he often stopped to witness to vendors. He was approached by several gunmen who offered him one last chance to rejoin the rebel movement, but Monchini refused. To the horror of surrounding witnesses the gunmen shot him at point blank range, escaping on foot as the fatally wounded Monchini fell to the ground.

'Within our group they constantly lived a life of challenge and commitment,' remembered Pablo Alcides, a young Christian leader who worked side-by-side with the two from the beginning of their born-again experience. 'Monchini once prayed that I would receive greater strength and fortitude. Their faith reached such an extreme that they truly denied themselves to follow Jesus Christ.'

Juan Carlos' mother still sells tortillas at the local market and her eyes betray the loss she carries within. 'He used to say that the road to God is hardest for people who don't want to follow Him, but for him it was the easiest thing because a total commitment to God meant that everything would turn out all right,' she recalled.

Evangelism efforts in El Salvador have been especially directed to the youth in recent years. With more than 50 per cent of the Latin American population under the age of 20, this young generation has been targeted as the single largest mission field to be reached in the eighties.

Says Church of God national youth director, Jose Elias Campos, 'We have 12,000 young people in our denomination alone. In 1985 we want to double that membership; and by encouraging other churches to do the same we believe we can reach at least 50 per cent of El Salvador's young people in this year alone.'

'One Reaching One' is the name of just one youth outreach programme out of the many that are in progress in El Salvador today. The country remains entirely free for whatever religious activities Christians may want to carry out. Churches are full; denominations have learned to co-operate one with another in a common cause; and the new martyrs of the Church have inspired the weak to be strong.

To emphasise this new direction for the Salvadoran church, the Christians have declared 1985 the 'Year of Renovation'. Although they have no adequate surveys that show exactly what percentage of the population now profess faith in Jesus Christ, national leaders believe that the single digit percentage of the seventies is no longer valid, as up to 20 per cent of the Salvadoran population today may claim Jesus Christ as Lord of their lives.

If this is true, then the Salvadoran wartime revival truly has made an historic impression on the country named after our Saviour.

7: A brighter tomorrow

By Dale W Kietzman

Costa Rica has traditionally been a hub of evangelical activities and a mecca for mission boards and inter-denominational commissions. The Missionary Spanish Language Institute cycles hundreds of prospects through its doors, and many stay in Costa Rica; or return to it after completing assignments elsewhere. This concentration of activity has spawned a total of at least twenty Bible institutes and seminaries in the country with the smallest population base and the smallest evangelical church membership in Central America.

The relatively modest church growth in Costa Rica seems puzzling in the light of this concentration of church leadership. Are there logical explanations for the apparent lack of response here?

One notable difference is that Costa Rica is the only Central American republic that still has an established church—the Roman Catholic Church, which has enjoyed a special status throughout the country's history. Government support of Catholic institutions, and its freedom from burdens applied to the Evangelicals, effectively relegates the Protestant congregations to a second-class status.

Costa Rica has also had the most stable democratic political tradition of any of these countries; a record which is unmatched anywhere in Latin America. The resulting freedom of movement and of expression probably accounts for the influx of foreign mission offices. It may also have allowed the churches, being free of some of the tensions experienced elsewhere, to be more at ease.

During 1984, evangelical leaders had adopted a prayer goal of seeing a great sense of unity among the various denominations and para-church activities in Costa Rica. There was some apparent success in this goal. According to the University Christian Students leader Sixto Porras: 'Today it is more unified than ever in the history of Costa Rica.'

But perhaps that new unity and sense of working together in a common cause comes from some fresh legal challenges that came to the fore in 1984. The Catholic Conference of Bishops had proposed an addition to the General Education Law that would assign to the Catholic Church the supervision of all religious education in the country, both formal and informal. They argued for this prerogative on the basis of their historical involvement in education in the country; on the fact that the state supported the church and its mission of evangelisation; and that education is an aspect of evangelisation.

Interestingly enough, Communist deputies have opposed this provision almost as much as Evangelicals, but not out of love of the one for the other. The general view of the left is that the Evangelicals are tools of the United States, as is proven by the regular financial support the missions and other agencies receive from North America.

Yet, despite these problems, Evangelicals continue to find San Jose as the most useful location for their base of operations in Central America (the competing location would be Guatemala City). It is not surprising, therefore, that many of the new evangelistic thrusts emanate from it to other parts of Latin America. Evangelism in Depth originated here, under Kenneth Strachan and the Latin American Mission. The Goodwill Caravans began in the minds of Costa Rican Christians.

Now a dramatic new evangelism concept has been added to that list. This is a co-ordinated, continent-wide, all-church, simultaneous evangelistic effort called 'Young Continent for Christ'.

The 'Young Continent' label is an apt one, with an estimated (mid-1984) 9,915,000 children under the age of 15 in the five Central American republics, a whopping 44 per cent of the total population of 22,400,000. According to Joseph Pent, president of Costa Rican-based Latin American Assistance, on the basis of a survey he had made, only five per cent of all missionaries and Christian workers in Latin America concentrated their efforts on the under-20 age group; this in spite of the fact that more than 50 per cent of all Latin Americans fall into this age bracket.

In 1980, leaders of youth ministries from throughout Central America and the Caribbean had gathered in Costa Rica to discuss the challenge revolutionary ideologies were making for the loyalties—and the lives—of the student population of the area. They received documented information that the guerrillas fighting the larger and smaller wars in Central America were frighteningly young, some known to be only nine years of age.

At the same time, they discovered, young people raised in the church were dropping out. They no longer found there adequate answers for the mounting social and economic problems seemingly flooding over Central America, and blocking all hope for their own futures.

One participant described the situation in Central America as being like an old stone bridge over which a growing flow of traffic is passing. 'When cracks appear in the bridge, they put up a sign saying, "Load Limit 10 Tons", but do nothing about the increasing flow of traffic.

'When more cracks appear, they put up another sign, "Load Limit 5 Tons" but still make no move to repair the bridge or stop the traffic flow.

'That's Central America. The old institutions are showing the strains of time; they can no longer respond to our needs in a modern world. But no changes occur. Meanwhile, we are in the midst of a population explosion. We lower expectations—nothing more. Some day that bridge will just explode and crumble.'

The 1980 meeting set up AME, the Alliance of Christian Student Movements of Latin America. Peruvian-born José Pent and Manuel Tijerino Silva, a Nicaraguan who was then pastor of the fast growing Christian Centre in Heredia, Costa Rica, were selected as co-ordinators, with Arturo Londono Marmolejo, a Colombian youth worker resident in Costa Rica, as the executive secretary.

Arturo Londono is himself almost a case study of the young people AME was designed to help. As a student in Colombia, he had been caught up in the campus revolutionary ferment. He was told he could mix his Christian convictions with Marxist ideology. Even though 'changing the system' might require violence, he had been induced to believe 'that suffering would stop and there would be more love and fellowship among people.'

Discovery from practical observation that such love and fellowship are not the products of violence, Arturo dedicated his life to student ministry.

'The reason we want to reach the young people is that they are the ones who bring about the changes in Latin America,' he explains. 'So if we can win them with the Gospel, then the changes that they will make are going to be more positive.

'We want to tell all the young people that there is a hope and that we should stop killing each other and start living for each other instead. Then they will be a part of a revolution of love, not of hate.'

Out of such commitment, the 'Young Continent for Christ' concept was born. Its appeal, while directed at young Christians to involve them to reach their friends, is also directed at pastors who, in the Latin congregations, hold the key for encouraging, training and directing their own young people to adopt the vision of the campaign.

And widespread participation will be needed. The leaders from Central America, with whom the plan originated, have set a goal of having 10,000,000 young people receive a personal witness by the end of 1985.

Joseph Pent expressed the burden of the others when he declared, 'We have accepted a new and pro- phetic vision of a young continent for Christ. The youth of Latin America are today's revolutionaries. We want to use Christian young people to evangelise the continent. They themselves are saying, we must "fight fire with fire" '.

That slogan, *fuego contra fuego* in Spanish, is reminiscent of Lenin's phrase that described how revolutionary change begins: 'From the spark, a flame.' In this case, these young leaders want to set back-fires of Spirit-directed evangelism to curb the spread of godless and misguided revolution.

The backers of Young Continent have travelled throughout Latin America, organising local committees and appointing reference people (*referentes*) in every country. Still, there is no organisation being built; each country develops its own programme, even its own name (in Brazil it is the 'One + One' campaign). The goal is to motivate the maximum number of denominations, organisations and local congregations to get involved, in their own way, toward this evangelism goal.

'We are not talking here about an isolated event in Latin America,' explains Pent. 'We are talking about a strategy to encourage every local church to use all means to reach as many as we can for Jesus Christ.'

'But the great thing about "Young Continent for Christ" ', notes Peter Gonzalez, the Mexican-born radio broadcaster who is a leading proponent of the movement, 'is that this is Latins reaching Latins for Christ. It is one-to-one evangelism on an unprecedented scale.'

The results of the campaign during 1984, the start-up year, have been encouraging. A four-day session of 'referentes' to review progress and plan toward the future, was held in Guatemala City in January, 1985. While no one is trying to keep a scorecard on conversions, and some countries have shown much larger results than others, it appears that at least one-third of the targeted 10,000,000 young people have received that personal witness of the Gospel which is the goal.

One of the first efforts in Costa Rica had included a rally by radio evangelist Hermano Pablo, who spoke on the campus of Costa Rica's National University at the invitation of Sixto Porras, the 'Young Continent for Christ' representative. The largely Marxist student body swarmed to the outdoor rally, in what was a first of its kind on campus, and the students responded warmly to his message.

That result was somewhat akin to the report of Chile's Christian Casanova. 'Once when I was preaching on a university campus, the students set fire to the stage on which I was standing. Suddenly I was surrounded by fire. But,' he continued, 'politicians are good motivators, and preachers should be, too. Regardless of what happens, if I don't see people coming to Christ when I've finished, then I've failed.'

Casanova, who is the founder of Chile's effective 'Revolution of Jesus Christ' movement, has used the impetus of Young Continent to forge perhaps the most aggressive strategy yet for reaching university students with the Gospel. He reported 40,000 new decisions during 1984.

Some of the other reports give an idea of the scope of the campaign and of the wide variety of methods being used. In Nicaragua, for instance, the 1984 theme, 'Win Nicaragua for Christ,' heralded an unprecedented mobilisation of the Church there, involving practically every member of the Christian community. The Church witnessed the dramatic conversion of 100,000 people throughout the country, many of whom found Jesus Christ through the effective ministry of the movie, 'Jesus'. Of the 350,000 Nicaraguans who viewed the film, 40,000 made decisions for Jesus Christ. Many of these are serving two-year terms in the Sandinista Army.

'When I speak about Nicaragua, I feel great sorrow and pain,' commented the Nicaraguan representative at the recent Guatemala meeting. 'How much I wish that we could have had a plan like 'Young Continent for Christ' several years ago.'

The Salvadoran 'referente' reported that 'God is using every situation to win others. If we did not have a civil crisis, the Church would not be growing in this way.'

Salvadoran leaders have grasped the vision of Young Continent and backed it with an 'Alliance for Prayer'. Each month the organising commission meets for prayer and planning of activities. Leaders estimate that at least 150,000 Salvadoran young people have heard the Gospel. Of these, 16,000 decisions were recorded in 1984, and 50 per cent of these will be baptised in the coming months. With the help of Open Doors, the World Home Bible League and the Salvadoran Bible Society, young people distributed 75,000 New Testaments throughout the country during personal and massive evangelistic activities in 1984.

During November and December of 1984, the organising committee in Costa Rica saturated the universities and secondary schools with 50,000 Bible portions distributed to the students. For one event, they invited a Christian Puerto Rican singer as the main attraction at a well promoted dinner meeting, for which the attendance goal was 700; 2,000 actually attended!

The Young Continent committee hopes to broadcast at least thirty additional youth-oriented radio progammes and several television programmes during 1985. They plan discipleship seminars, evangelistic campaigns, and hundreds of film showings. Five hundred murals have been painted, and banners hung in key areas around the capital city, in conjunction with the United Nations' 1985 International Year of Youth theme.

'Dare to Win 10 Million' is a slogan used in

Guatemala. 'We have broadcast this message over radio, television and in the national press,' reported Guatemala's Young Continent representative. 'If you could only read some of the letters we have received!'

The committee then held twenty-six conventions and six training sessions for youth leaders nationwide in 1984 to share the vision of winning today's troubled youth for Christ.

'We have plastered the country with stickers proclaiming our goal and printed logos on T-shirts worn by Christian youth as they set out to win their friends for Jesus. We can point to thousands of solid new believers who are the fruit of this year's evangelistic effort.'

The Guatemalan leader also reported New Testaments were distributed among military personnel, and other government institutions have called the Young Continent office in Guatemala City requesting literature and assistance for their youth.

'Although we realise that the students and young people in our cities must be reached, we are also very burdened for the vast Indian population of our country.' Special attention is being given to Quiche province, an area ravaged by intense guerrilla activity in recent years.

It could well be that on this one vision of a 'Young Continent for Christ' hangs the future of Latin America. Certainly these fired-up young people are the church leaders of tomorrow. And they are very much aware of the role they are playing in the spiritual battle now in progress, in which the prize is not just Central America, but the world.

In Guatemala, the Peruvian 'referente', Manuel Paredes, talked of their response to Satan's strategy:

'The world is uniting to create an offensive against the Christians. God is looking for unity and integrity. Satan wants to divide the leaders, those committed to a cause, because when leaders are divided, they lose their authority and effectiveness. We must show the power and authority of what it means to follow Jesus Christ. Let's learn to live differently, to be fully committed, whether we're living under governments of the right or the left.'

Peter Gonzalez adds, 'What is important is that the young people of Latin America get to hear that life does not consist just of a choice between left or right. There is a third choice: the way of Jesus Christ.'

Table 1. Central America in figures

	Costa Rica	El Salvador	Guatemala	Honduras	Nicaragua
Mid-1984 population*	2,500,000	4,800,000	8,000,000	4,200,000	2,900,000
Area in square miles	19,575	8,260	42,300	43,277	50,193
Population density: number of people per square mile	128	581	190	97	58
Natural annual increase	2.7%	2.6%	3.5%	3.4%	3.6%
Projected population in A.D.2000	3,400,000	7,800,000	12,400,000	7,000,000	4,800,000
Per cent population under age 15	36%	45%	44%	47%	48%
Years life expectancy at birth	72	64	59	58	56
Present urban population	48%	39%	39%	37%	53%
Per cent rural population	52%	61%	61%	63%	47%
Per capita GNP 1982 (US$)	$1,280	$700	$1,130	$600	$920

*Mid-1984 population data is drawn from the 1984 World Population Data Sheet of the Population Reference Bureau, Inc., Washington, D.C.

Table 2. The Protestant Church in Central America*

	Costa Rica	El Salvador	Guatemala	Honduras	Nicaragua
Percentage of Protestants	8%	7%	21%	8%	12%
Church members	44,829	98,224	286,129	77,054	78,387
Total community	141,000	295,000	1,161,600	280,000	276,000
Number of congregations	725	2,059	6,216	1,869	1,531
Number of denominations	65	80	200	40	75

*These data are taken or extrapolated from *Central America and the Caribbean*, edited by Clifton L Holland, vol. 4 of *World Christianity* (Monrovia, California: Mission Advanced Research and Communications, 1981). The data for individual countries were compiled between 1976 and 1980, and the percentages apply to the then current population figures.

If you wish to receive *regular information* about *new books*, please send your name and address to:

London Bible Warehouse
PO Box 123
Basingstoke
Hants RG23 7NL

Name _____

Address _____

_____

_____

_____

I am especially interested in:

☐ Biographies
☐ Fiction
☐ Christian living
☐ Issue related books
☐ Academic books
☐ Bible study aids
☐ Children's books
☐ Music
☐ Other subjects

P.S. If you have ideas for new Christian Books or other products, please write to us too!

Other Marshall Pickering Paperbacks

THROUGH DAVID'S PSALMS

Derek Prince

Derek Prince, internationally known Bible teacher and scholar, draws on his understanding of the Hebrew language and culture, and a comprehensive knowledge of Scripture, to present 101 meditations from the Psalms.
Each of these practical and enriching meditations is based on a specific passage and concludes with a faith response. They can be used either for personal meditation or for family devotions. They are intended for all those who want their lives enriched or who seek comfort and encouragement from the Scriptures.

LOVING GOD

Charles Colson

Loving God is the very purpose of the believer's life, the vocation for which he is made. However loving God is not easy and most people have given little real thought to what the greatest commandment really means.
Many books have been written on the individual subjects of repentence, Bible study, prayer, outreach, evangelism, holiness and other elements of the Christian life. In **Loving God**, Charles Colson draws all these elements together to look at the entire process of growing up as a Christian.
Combining vivid illustrations with straightforward exposition he shows how to live out the Christian faith in our daily lives. **Loving God** provides a real challenge to deeper commitment and points the way towards greater maturity.